Praise for *Resilient Black Girl*

"Informative, engaging and encouraging—*Resilient Black Girl* is all of these things, and more. It is a very timely and powerful book for our Black girls and girls of color to reclaim their confidence and be beacons of courage and hope for generations to come."

—Shanicia Boswell, founder of the Black Moms blog

"*Resilient Black Girl* is a critical and powerful tool for our young Black girls. The activities and lessons offered are fundamental in shaping them into the powerful Black women they need to be in our world today."

—Mike the Poet, author of *Dear Woman*

"Society is known to have an erosive effect on Black girls' confidence. Luckily enough, *Resilient Black Girl* equips them with the knowledge and confidence to not only reverse that effect but overpower it."

—Karen Arrington, author of *Your Next Level Life*

RESILIENT BLACK GIRL

RESILIENT BLACK GIRL

52 Weeks of Anti-Racist Activities for Black Joy and Resilience

M.J. FIEVRE

CORAL GABLES

Resilient Black Girl: 52 Weeks of Anti-Racist Activities for Black Joy and Resilience

Library of Congress Cataloging-in-Publication number: 2021941080
ISBN: (print) 978-1-64250-654-9, (ebook) 978-1-64250-655-6
BISAC category code YAN001000, YOUNG ADULT NONFICTION /
Activity Books

Printed in the United States of America

Table of Contents

This Is Your Time to Shine

Welcome to fifty-two weeks of living with intention. *Resilient Black Girl: 52 Weeks of Anti-Racist Activities for Black Joy and Resilience* was designed to help you get motivated to make real changes to your life and your way of thinking.

I grew up in Haiti, a Black nation led by Black people. The people of Haiti do not experience racism as it exists in the United States; what presents itself mostly there is colorism (prejudice against individuals with a darker skin tone, among people of the same ethnic or racial group). Imagine my shock and surprise when I immigrated to the United States and, on top of having to deal with a new language and culture, discovered that I was often singled out for the color of my skin, whether it was a group of kids who threw a milkshake at me, or a college professor who assumed I was lazy because I fell behind in my work trying to keep up with the language.

Throughout my years working as an educator, I've seen firsthand the kind of damage that racism can do to a young person's spirit. The effects of racism are real and damaging. I've seen many promising students become disengaged and withdrawn because of racist incidents. I know the perils of the school to prison pipeline which disproportionately affects Black and Brown kids. I've also seen the real beauty of students who overcame the struggles of racism and became strong, confident, and comfortable in their own power, and were able to become successful in their classes and their lives.

Resilient Black Girl is a book about the realities of being Black. It leads Black girls and young Black women to a better understanding of the effects of racism and teaches them how to navigate various spaces. This book is a guide filled with activities and prompts that encourage empowerment and self-reliance, providing you with tools for combating racism in your daily life. There is no doubt, you are powerful, but unfortunately, you'll face microaggressions and outright racism in your daily life. *Resilient Black Girl* will help empower you to be brave, face the challenges of oppression, and rely on yourself.

Learn to:

- **Understand and combat racism and microaggressions in your daily life.** Once you identify how racism affects your physical and mental health, you can love and take care of yourself.
- **Become a leader in your community.** To become a well-rounded Black girl is to become an important member of your society. This journal and activity workbook guides you through achieving your personal and public goals.
- **Be brave, empowered, and self-reliant.** Being a Black girl comes with many gifts, one being resiliency. While you are strong and can overcome anything, be kind to yourself.

I've paired twenty-six lessons in anti-racism with fifty-two writing exercises. These exercises will open your mind to the world around you, and the world within you. As you go through these activities, keep in mind that you are developing a practice, a foundation of mindful activity you can build on for the future. These activities don't have to stop after the year is over. I hope journaling and anti-racist awareness will become part of your daily rituals for life.

The writing exercises were adapted from narrative therapy techniques that have been shown to increase confidence and lower anxiety and depression as well as increase motivation and self-knowledge, something every resilient Black girl needs. Being resilient isn't something we are born with; it's a learned trait. And sometimes you snap a little. It's okay to break down, but getting back up is what makes you resilient and powerful.

The anti-racist chapters are part of an education every Black girl should have in the truth of the situation-at-large. They will equip you with the knowledge you need to navigate these trying times in a society that's not built to accommodate Blackness. These lessons will help you understand how our society works and how you can fight back against inequity and injustice in a safe and productive way. You *can* fight back against injustice. It's a battle many brave warrior women are fighting all over the world.

As you start this journey, I'm excited to know that you will be exploring and learning about yourself and the world. I hope you enjoy the process and come out of the year ready to take on whatever life has to offer you in terms of fulfilling your dreams. Remember to dream big!

WRITING PROMPTS:

Gaining Perspective

These exercises will help you review your life and gain a different kind of perspective on your past, which can help you project into a brighter future for yourself. The word "perspective" implies clear vision and understanding, so when you complete these entries, keep that in mind. Part of what makes journaling such a positive activity is that it teaches you about yourself, who you are, and what makes you tick. Getting to know yourself is a process that many of us don't think to engage in, but it's one that will help seal your individuality and create a better understanding of your foundational traits.

WEEK 1: CREATE A TIMELINE.

For this exercise you'll be asked to create a visual timeline of your life with all the most significant moments illustrated. An illustrated timeline is useful because it gives you a clear progression of your life in pictures that you can easily look at to see how you've grown as a person.

First, think of all the most significant moments in your life and write them down on a timeline that starts with your first memory, like starting school, moving, making a friend, or having an experience with an influential person in your life. Draw the memory as you remember it happening or pick an image from the memory and draw that. Continue with the rest of your timeline, drawing the most important or special moments to you, until you have a visual representation of your life laid out in images. You may want to use art paper for this exercise or oversized poster board to give you enough room to draw out the memories. You can also project into the future by drawing a future timeline with images of what you hope to achieve in the future years. This is an activity you can do in one sitting, or one you can come back to as memories come to you. It's up to you to decide how long you want to spend on it, but it's probably a good idea to plan at least an hour for your first session of drawing memories.

WEEK 2: MY LIFE STORY

In this exercise, I'm asking you to write your life story from the beginning, with your first memories. You can use your visual timeline as a guide to help you remember the most significant memories, but delve deeper into the story and really write about all the little nuances of life that we tend to take for granted. Expect to spend several hours on this exercise as it's asking you to recapture your whole life story, and again, it's up to you whether you want to break this exercise down into shorter periods or work through it all at once. Remember to capture as many images as you can, and project into the future to tell your life story as you hope it pans out over the next few years.

PART I: SANCTUARY

Her Name is Aiyana

Aiyana Stanley-Jones's shooting death sparked public outrage a decade before the Black Lives Matter movement became prevalent. To understand Black Lives Matter and what the movement stands for, it's important to know what happened to Aiyana Stanley-Jones. It's also important to understand here that when we reference Black Lives Matter in this book, we are emphasizing the phrase and the movement, not the organization that was later formed by Alicia Garza, Patrisse Cullors, and Opal Tometi.

Just after midnight on the night of May 16, 2010, a half-dozen masked Detroit Police officers from the Special Response Team approached the lower level of a duplex where seven-year-old Aiyana Stanley-Jones was asleep on the couch with her grandmother. Tagging along with the police unit was a film crew working for A&E's reality program *The First 48*. The police approached the duplex with their guns drawn, even though they had been alerted that children lived in the building and the lawn out front was marked with toys that had been left out. Police threw a flash-bang grenade into the apartment and then kicked the door open. The grenade landed close enough to Aiyana that it set her blanket on fire. Officer Joseph Weekley, the lead commander of the police unit entered the apartment and fired one shot. It struck Aiyana in the head and exited her neck, killing her.

The killing sparked an outcry after it was reported. The officers were there in search of a suspect on the upper floor of the duplex, not the first. Joseph Weekley was first charged with involuntary manslaughter and reckless endangerment with a gun. His first trial ended in a mistrial. During his retrial, the judge dismissed the involuntary manslaughter charge against him, leaving him with only the reckless endangerment charge. The second trial also ended in a mistrial. Prior to his third trial, a prosecutor cleared

Weekley of the reckless endangerment charge, leaving him free from prosecution.

In the aftermath of her death, calls were made for an Attorney General investigation, Reverend Al Sharpton spoke at her funeral, and a small vigil was held, but Aiyana never received justice for her death.

What We Learned from Aiyana Stanley-Jones:

- Black people are not safe, not even in the comfort of their own homes or the familiarity of their own neighborhoods.
- Many people see Black people as threats rather than as human beings.
- We are linked in our struggles as Black people, and the systemic oppression that affects us is also linked.
- Anti-Black bias is widespread and implicit, but our legal system lacks the power and balance needed to deliver any measure of justice to the Black community.
- Liberation will only come when Black-centric concerns are addressed and when we build a world where Black lives actually matter and are protected.

Shortly after midnight on March 13, 2020, a team of Louisville, KY policemen, executing a no-knock warrant, used a battering ram to break down the door of twenty-six-year-old Breonna Taylor's apartment. After a brief confrontation, the police opened fire. Ms. Taylor died after she was shot at least eight times. In the aftermath of her killing, Taylor's mother, Tamika Palmer, told the *Courier Journal,* "She had a whole plan on becoming a nurse and buying a house and then starting a family. Breonna had her head on straight, and she was a very decent person. She didn't deserve this. She wasn't that type of person." Ms. Taylor, a paramedic, had no prior criminal history. The police had executed the search warrant on the wrong apartment.

We're Not Safe, but We Can Be.

Since Aiyana's death, many more Black boys and girls have died unjustly at the hands of people who mistook them for criminals. The chances of being shot during a police encounter are much greater for Black people. This can cause a great deal of unsettling anxiety and fear.

End-Of-Life Reflections

It can be uncomfortable to think of your own death and the end of your life, but we all reach that point in our lives sometime, and thinking about death now can help prepare you to live a better life in the intervening years.

The following prompts are about empathy, given that many Black and Brown kids are taken from this world too soon. These exercises are NOT meant to ask you to imagine yourself a victim of police brutality or gun violence. Writing a eulogy, for example, provides an opportunity to consider what we would like our lives to reflect to the world. How can we maximize the time we have in this world? If we consider how we want to be remembered in our passing, that can guide our actions while living.

WEEK 3: EULOGY

This exercise asks you to write your own eulogy. Ask yourself how important an occasion this will be to the people who attend the funeral. Will they remember it even twenty years after it has passed? Who will you have made a difference to by the time your own funeral comes around, and in what ways? Who will survive you and what will you have meant to them? Be sure to write some of the accomplishments you hope to achieve and think of the ones you accomplished already. Write those in there too.

WEEK 4: PAST/PRESENT

In this exercise you'll look at a traumatic event from your past from two different perspectives: past tense and present tense. The idea behind this exercise is to see how viewing the incident from a different perspective reframes the story. Start by writing about the event in past tense, or from your current perspective. Don't think too much about what you're writing, just write. Now set it aside and come back to this exercise when you've had time to clear your head. When you are ready, rewrite the experience from present tense, or by re-entering the incident and reliving it. Ask yourself the following questions: How are the two versions of the event different? Which one has more sensory detail? Are the voices different? Is the level of detail different? Which one has a narrower perspective, and which takes a wider stance?

Talking About Racism

In 2016, a young man named Brian Crooks wrote a social media post detailing his experiences with racism. It resounded with many other Black people and went viral and resonated with many people who have had similar experiences. Throughout this book, I will be sharing parts of Brian's story to illustrate different aspects of racism you should recognize.

In this excerpt of Brian Crooks' story, which he publicly shared on social media, he relates the frustration of being hassled by the police regularly, and how his parents had prepared him for these encounters. He writes, "My parents had told me how to act when pulled over by the police, so of course I was all 'Yes sir, no sir' every time it happened. That didn't stop them from asking me to step out of the car so they could pat me down or search for drugs, though. I didn't have a drop of alcohol until I was twenty-one, but by that point I was an expert at breathalyzers and field sobriety tests."

How to Approach Your Parents About Racism

"The Talk" is a series of conversations you should have with your parents and other adults that aims to keep you safe and free from harm. You should be having these conversations regularly so that the message of "The Talk" is reinforced in your mind. Some of the things you might hear in "The Talk" include: Don't go into "that" neighborhood. Don't resist arrest. Don't leave home without your ID. Don't touch anything in the store if you aren't going to purchase it. Don't leave a store without having a bag for your purchase and a receipt. Don't go out in a crowd. Don't loiter. And so forth...

You may have already had a version of "The Talk" with your parents and are familiar with the ins and outs of discussing racism with them. If you've already started having "The Talk," you probably know how it was uncomfortable at first to discuss racism with your parents, but you should also see that as it becomes a part of your life, you grow more comfortable with opening up. You should ask yourself how "The Talk" is helping, and if there are things you haven't felt comfortable discussing with your parents about racism.

Many parents have a difficult time broaching the subject of racism with their kids. Talking to your parents about racism can be a difficult process, especially if one (or both) of your parents is not Black. They may think that their love is enough to keep you safe and secure. They may feel like they are preserving your innocence by ignoring racism and not discussing it with you, but ignoring racism doesn't make it go away, and the ability to have open, direct conversations about racism with your parents will help you have other difficult discussions with them more easily.

You may find it is easier to talk to your friends about difficult subjects, and that is completely normal, but it's important for you to be in tune with your parents and to keep them updated on what you are going through so they can provide you the kind of support you need. It's important to remember that talking about race isn't a one-time discussion; it's something you should be able to talk about frequently, because it impacts you frequently. Here are some tips for broaching the difficult topic of racism with your parents:

- **Talk to them about your day-to-day life.** It will be easier to talk to your parents about racism if you are talking to them about other things, like how you did on your biology exam or what the dog did during his last walk. Let your parents into your life as much as you can.

- **Know what you want out of the conversation.** You may want your parents to just listen without giving any support or advice. You may want their permission to do something. You may need their support or advice. Or you may need their guidance and assistance. Whatever it is, knowing how you want the conversation to proceed will help you.
- **Identify your feelings.** Knowing how you feel about the topic going in will help your parents know how to react. You can say, "I saw something on the internet and it's making me angry (or sad, or confused)."
- **Pick a good time to talk.** Ask them, "Mom and Dad, I have something I need to discuss with you. Is this a good time to talk?" Your parents might ask you to wait for a time when they are prepared to give you their undivided attention.
- **Be clear and direct.** Be as up front as possible with your parents. Tell them you want to discuss racism and why you're bringing it up.
- **Be honest.** It's a good idea to be honest all the time. If you are, your parents will believe you if you tell them something shocking or surprising.
- **Try to understand their point of view.** Your parents will be much more likely to listen to your side if you are willing to hear them out.
- **Consider finding another trusted adult.** If you are unable to talk to your parents about race, consider finding someone else who will be able to talk to you like a clergy member or school counselor. Remember, your parents are human too.

Use Hand Signals for Difficult Conversations.

Teach your parents and siblings hand signals for difficult conversations. Sometimes conversations can get so intense you can lose your ability to speak clearly. If that happens, these hand signals can communicate what you are feeling:

- **Closed fist:** This means the conversation has gotten too uncomfortable and I can't continue.
- **One finger raised:** I am uncomfortable, and I need some breathing room before I can continue.
- **Two fingers raised:** I am feeling a little uncomfortable, but I want to try to continue.
- **Three fingers raised:** I am confused about what I'm feeling.
- **Four fingers raised:** I feel comfortable enough to continue.
- **Five fingers raised, open palm:** Keep going!

Beyond "The Talk"

There is a lot you can do to make things easier for your parents in terms of learning about racism and just communicating openly with your parents in general. Here are a few pointers:

- **Don't roll your eyes when your parents want to talk.** Try to be open in communication with your parents, and really listen to what they are trying to tell you. This is a difficult stage when you are trying to gain more independence from your parents and the impulse is to back away from them as you gain more freedom. Your parents are likely having a rough time with all the changes too, but remember that most parents have already lived through some of the most challenging historical incidents and can offer great insight and wisdom if you are willing to listen. Keep that in mind when you are in conversation with them and be respectful.

- **Ask questions.** If you don't understand something your parents are saying, ask questions. Asking questions is a great way to open a conversation as well. Allow your parents to ask you questions as well. And really think of an answer when they ask. The typical response a parent gets from a teenager is "I dunno." Be a little more thoughtful with your answers to their questions, even if it's difficult.

- **Develop media literacy.** Learn how to find information on the internet, and how to check to see if a source is reliable. This way you won't have to rely on anyone to keep you informed. Watch videos of protests or marches from the past and compare how similar they are to what's happening today. Watch documentaries about the civil right era so that you have a good handle on the history of activism.

- **Avoid stereotypes.** They're not funny, even if you're just joking. Stereotypes are harmful. People are individuals with individual qualities. Try to see the nuances beyond stereotypes. One good way to root out stereotypical thinking, even if it's not conscious, is to take the Implicit Associations Test(s) at implicit.harvard.edu/implicit/education.html. These anonymous online tests measure implicit bias toward different groups of people. Some of the tests include: Age, Disability, Race, Gender, etc. These tests are good at measuring implicit bias, which you might not even be aware you have.

- **Learn about activism.** Find out what organizations are working in your area to make change and how you can participate. Get involved with a local social justice organization or an after-school community center program aimed at promoting social justice.

- **Learn about history.** Read books and watch documentaries on the history of racism and the struggle for Civil Rights. Educate yourself about racism by learning about history, and talk to the elders in your community. This will give you an understanding of how actions lead directly to consequences, both good and bad.

- **Take a stand.** On the Wall of Tolerance in the Civil Rights Memorial Center, visitors have hung their signed pledges to work against hate, injustice and intolerance. You can sign a pledge with your parents too. The pledge reads: "I pledge to take a stand against hate, injustice and intolerance. I will work in my daily life for justice, equality and human rights— the ideals for which the Civil Rights martyrs died." All you have to do is write down the pledge and sign and date it.

Write a Letter to Someone

A lot of people of color are tired—tired of being unseen and misunderstood. As a writing coach and writing teacher, I've found that when given the opportunity, many of my students open up in their writing and express emotions they may not have even realized they had. Writing a letter to someone you know can be cathartic in many ways. There are a million opportunities we all miss daily to express our appreciation or joy at knowing someone. There are also harder emotions to express that we balk at, including anger, disappointment, disgust, and sadness. Black girls in general are often taught to keep their emotions in check and not express themselves clearly and directly. This can lead to repressed emotions, which aren't healthy for you.

For Weeks 5 and 6, I'm asking you to write letters that you don't have to send, though you may choose to do so if you feel it would be helpful. Don't worry about that right now. Just focus on getting out whatever you need to release. You can figure out later whether you want the person you're writing to actually read what you've written.

WEEK 5: COMPOSE A LETTER TO A LOVED ONE.

In this exercise you'll compose a letter to someone you love. It can be a cherished family member or a friend who means the world to you, a coach, or a mentor. Or it might be someone else who has made your life better by being there for you when you've needed them. The goal of this exercise is to express gratitude to the person for the light they have brought into your life. Take a moment to breathe deeply and reflect on the different ways this person has made a difference in your life. Now make a list of the ways they have helped you. It might be a big moment like listening to you when you were hurt and being patient when you needed an ear. Maybe they helped you through a rough time. It might be many small things like the way they always smile at you when you greet them, and that makes you feel appreciated and loved. Whatever it is, try to list ten things. If you can come up with more items for your list, even better!

Once you have a list, start writing your letter. Don't stop to think too much about what you're saying. You can always revise it for clarity after the first draft. Just write. Let the person know that you are grateful for the many ways they have been a part of your life. Be specific with how they have helped you. It might be something like, "When you smile at me, I feel like I belong in a way I don't often feel with other people." Or whatever it is you want to express to them. Try to write without stopping for ten minutes.

When you are done with the draft, read it over. Is it clear enough? If not, you can always go back and rewrite the letter from beginning to end, clarifying the points you want to make to the intended recipient of the letter. Go slower on the revision. Read parts of the letter out loud to yourself. How does it make you feel to express gratitude to the person? Are there other things you wish you had said to the person that you haven't been bold enough to say? Remember you don't have to send this letter if you don't want to. Be bold now. Say what's in your heart.

When you are done writing the letter, put it in an envelope and set it aside for at least a week. Go back to the letter after a week and look it over. Is there anything you'd like to add? If so, add it now. Then decide whether you want to share the letter with your loved one. You can mail it to them, give it in person, or read it to them over the phone or in a video chat. Or you can keep it tucked away, safe, and hold the feelings you have for the person in your heart. But remember, gratitude is a wonderful thing to share.

WEEK 6: CREATE A POSTCARD TO EXPRESS YOUR FEELINGS.

This exercise combines art therapy techniques with writing therapy. Sometimes a person does or says something that triggers negative emotions, and it can be difficult to express those emotions to the other person without feeling vulnerable and exposed. This exercise is another where you do not have to send the recipient of the postcard the finished item if you don't feel comfortable. It may help you just to release some negative emotions and move forward.

To start, cut out a postcard sized black piece of poster board. If you don't have poster board, try to find some thick paper. Now, take some deep breaths and think about how the person you are addressing the postcard to made you feel. What exactly did they do? Take a few minutes to reflect on what happened and on the accompanying emotions.

Using whatever colorful items you have handy, such as crayons, colored pens or pencils, or watercolors, draw an image of your emotions on one side of the postcard. Don't worry about how it looks, just create an image that represents what you are feeling. Allow yourself to revisit the emotions as you create the image and feel yourself releasing them and letting them go.

On the other side of the postcard write a short note naming the emotions and why you felt them. Be specific. It might be something like, "Dear Mom, it makes me feel angry and humiliated when you criticize what I choose to wear in front of other people. I like my own style, and want to dress myself in a way that expresses who I am." It may be something else completely, but the point is to name the emotions and why you have been feeling them.

When you are done with the postcard, do some more deep breathing, and feel yourself releasing the emotions attached to the image. Set the postcard aside in a safe place where it is secure from prying eyes for at least a week. After the week go back and look at the image. Does it still provoke the same emotions in you as when you first created it? Have your feelings about the event changed at all? How about your feelings about the person who triggered the emotions?

Depending on how you're feeling, there are a couple of different options for you in terms of what to do with the postcard after the week is up. If your emotions are more settled, you might want to rip it up and throw it away or bury it in the backyard. If the same problem is still an issue, you may want to communicate what you are feeling with the person you wrote to in the postcard exercise. It's entirely up to you. You have the power.

How Racism Affects You

It is a "no-brainer" that racism affects you, but professionals have also weighed in on the issue. In 2019, The American Academy of Pediatrics issued a policy statement that referred to racism as a "socially transmitted disease," in part, because children in minority groups are subject to chronic stress. They noted that higher levels of chronic stress cause changes in stress hormones, which leads to inflammation, which is a marker for chronic diseases and autoimmune disorders like heart disease, asthma, and diabetes. Changes to a mother's level of stress hormones during pregnancy can even impact her developing infant, leading to higher infant mortality risk and lower birth weights.

Minority children are more likely to live in lower income homes with greater rates of unemployment, which can affect their access to quality healthcare, education, and decent housing. But the problem of racism is still present in higher income communities, where minority kids are more likely to be punished at school, and less likely to be offered special education for learning disabilities. Teachers are also more likely to underestimate minority kids, which doesn't give them the needed impetus to push harder and try to achieve more. They are more likely to be suspended for behavior problems and have a higher rate of absenteeism.

No matter how hard they try, your parents cannot protect you from racist incidents. Even if you never experience a racist encounter directly, you are likely to see one of the many videos online of Black men and women being killed violently—and that will likely affect you. Even witnessing racism secondhand has a tremendous impact and can lead to a host of physical and mental health issues. Racism is a socially transmitted illness that should be a major public health concern. But it's often not seen as such.

To further complicate the problem of racism and health, Black people are less likely to have adequate access to medical care or are poorly/under treated when they do seek help. They may have trouble locating a healthcare professional with cultural sensitivity to the issues they are struggling with. Lack of adequate insurance can be a barrier for many people who need help but cannot afford it. In some communities, including Afro-Latinx and Afro-Caribbean communities, there may be a language barrier. There is also a pervasive stigma among many Black people associated with seeking help for mental illnesses or discussing painful emotions, so even if a problem is identified, it can go untreated. Some studies have shown that many Black people are afraid of being perceived as weak or crazy for seeking out mental health assistance.

Self-Exploration

As a Black girl, you'll be stressed out, you'll face trials and tribulations. I've struggled myself with issues of anxiety and depression and understanding my triggers has gone a long way to helping me heal my mental health. Part of the process of learning about my triggers was learning about myself. Getting to know yourself is an important activity. Think about the early days of your closest relationships. How much time and energy did you spend getting to know the other person? Now, think about this question: How well do you know yourself? If you aren't sure, these exercises will help you develop a better understanding and knowledge of yourself.

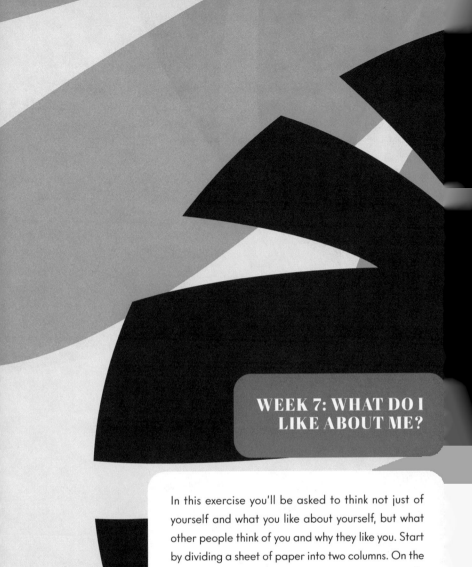

WEEK 7: WHAT DO I LIKE ABOUT ME?

In this exercise you'll be asked to think not just of yourself and what you like about yourself, but what other people think of you and why they like you. Start by dividing a sheet of paper into two columns. On the right side write down all the qualities other people have told you possess. Then, on the left side of the paper write down all the qualities you admire in yourself. Once you've written down all the qualities you can think of for both lists compare them and write about any differences between how others perceive you and how you perceive yourself. What major differences do you see?

WEEK 8: WHAT MAKES ME, ME?

In this exercise you'll be asked to look at yourself closely and find words that best describe you. To start, draw an outline of your body on a sheet of paper. Next, write down words that describe you on the drawing of yourself. Write as many as you can as fast as you can without stopping to think much. Next look over the words you brainstormed on the picture of your body. How many of them accurately describe you? Are you surprised with how many ideas you came up with? Write about the defining characteristics that make you, you. Lastly, write about the things in your life that have a positive impact on your sense of well-being. How many of these are internally driven?

The Physical Toll of Racism

The American Psychological Association (APA) reports that the constant stress of racism is a serious physical concern. It triggers a response in your adrenal glands which releases stress hormones including cortisol. According to the APA, "The chronic condition of stress was selected because of its prevalence and impact on health within health disparity population groups (e.g., people of color), and their high association with many other chronic diseases." Increased cortisol levels in your blood have been linked to:

- Insomnia
- Autoimmune diseases
- Heart disease
- High blood pressure
- Diabetes
- Obesity
- Weakened immune response
- Gastrointestinal disorders
- Respiratory infections
- Inflammatory conditions

The toll that racism takes on you has a real, damaging physical effect, but there are methods of dealing with it that can help you shake off the negative effects of racism. Physical exercise is one method that works. I find that it helps to take a walk in your bare feet and connect with the earth, or to dance in a way that connects me with my ancestors. Even just shaking your limbs out to loosen up the tension can be helpful.

WRITING PROMPTS:

Let It Out!

Seeping into our minds, racism often takes a physical and mental toll. The danger with the constant exposure to microaggressions is that we can internalize those thought patterns that stem from racism, and they can become part of our inner dialogue. We all have an inner dialogue that can turn caustic at times and erode our hard-won self-esteem. It's time for you to take control over that inner dialogue and change the things you tell yourself, from hyper-critical nagging to a more supportive, encouraging voice. You'll find you can do a lot more if you are supportive of your own efforts and kinder to yourself.

The next exercises ask you to deal directly with your inner critic and the negative thought patterns that slow you down or prevent you from living a healthy life.

WEEK 9: CALL OUT YOUR THOUGHTS.

It can be hard to notice negative, critical thoughts if you don't pay attention to what you are telling yourself. It's easy to let the inner critic rage in the background while you go about your day. To begin this exercise, take a notebook with you wherever you go during the course of a day. Pay attention to your inner voice, and when you hear it talking trash to you write those thoughts down, no matter how painful they are. Are these things you would say to your best friend? If not, why are you saying them to yourself? When it comes to self-care and self-love in conjunction with managing our thoughts, it's important that we are kind to ourselves, which may include combating self-criticism with a gentler approach.

WEEK 10: CHALLENGE YOUR THOUGHTS.

After you've discovered patterns of negative thought during Week 9, it's time to challenge them. Ask yourself the following questions about the thoughts you've written down: Is that a true thought? Can it factually be proven to be true? Is there a more positive way of speaking to myself? What's a more realistic way of dealing with myself in this situation? Write your answers down. In addition to acknowledging negative thoughts and reducing one's mental space for them, it's important to replace these negative thoughts with positive ones.

The Mental Toll of Racism

Raced-based traumatic stress injury has been defined as an emotional or physical pain (or the threat of emotional or physical pain) caused by racism. Harassment and discrimination cause stress to both your mind and your body, and early warning signs of racial trauma include body aches, fatigue, anxiety, depression, and difficulty sleeping.

Depression and anxiety are common aftereffects of racism, along with racial trauma, which manifests similarly to post-traumatic stress disorder (PTSD). In the acute stage of racial trauma, the symptoms progress to the point that they interfere with a person's ability to work or attend school. Signs of acute racial trauma include:

- Hypervigilance
- Heightened emotional states
- Depression
- Anxiety
- Persistent intrusive memories or thoughts
- Lack of appetite
- Increased startle response
- Physical exhaustion
- Self-destructive behaviors such as drug or alcohol abuse or careless risk-taking
- Migraines
- Outbursts of anger
- Nightmares
- Emotional numbness
- Difficulty concentrating
- Flashbacks

- Avoidant behaviors or dissociation
- Mental exhaustion

The chronic stress of dealing with racism can have a tragic effect: an increase in suicide rates among Black youth. Suicide is the second highest leading cause of death among all adolescents across every ethnic group after accidents, but the trends for Black youth are especially disturbing. Suicide rates are higher among Black teens than any other group, and Black kids (even those as young as five to eleven years old) are more likely to use more fatal means in their attempt. A victim of bullying, ten-year-old Ashawnty Davis, was found dead by suicide, hanging in a closet at home.

The rise in suicides among Black youth can be attributed to several factors including an increased internalization of racism and bullying, and a decline in the coping mechanisms available. Internalization of racism occurs when one begins to believe there is something personally flawed about themselves, and they begin to believe there is something wrong with who they are as a person, even beyond the racial difference. Black girls, in particular, often report feelings of hopelessness and depression, which can lead to an increase in suicidal ideation.

Be on the Lookout for the Signs of Depression.

The constant barrage of outright racism from classmates, implicit bias from educators, and microaggressions that students face can leave them traumatized if it's unchecked. It is critical for you to be on the lookout for signs of depression, which include physical complaints (headaches, stomach aches, etc.), loss of appetite, irritability, anger, and sleep disturbances, to name a few. If you or one of your friends is depressed, it is imperative that you seek immediate medical help or at least seek out an adult who can help you.

Sometimes we mask our depression by trying to manage the comments we hear from others. Black girls often hear that they are less pretty than their white classmates, that they don't have good hair, and rather than accept a different set of defining characteristics for what is "beautiful," we try to fit in by straightening our hair with harsh chemicals or by buying lightening creams to make our skin appear lighter and more "attractive" according to white/European standards. It's much easier to learn to love yourself just the way you are than it is to try to fit someone else's ideal of beauty.

In Afro-Caribbean communities, anti-Black racism, and other forms of systemic oppression, can break our young people too, and the fact that mental health is still taboo in many families puts our Black children at risk—you might be reluctant to look for help and risk challenging the established concept of Black resilience. Be courageous and consider the help of a mental health professional, preferably one with the same cultural background, who will understand some of the stigma associated with depression within Afro-Caribbean spaces. Depression in Afro-Caribbean culture often looks much different than it does in other cultures, and it can be easy to miss the problem, or dismiss it as something else.

If you are exhibiting signs of acute anxiety or depression, expressing thoughts of suicide, or acting out in dangerous ways, it is imperative that you let your parents know and ask them to seek professional help with a licensed therapist right away. In a crisis, you can call the Suicide Prevention Helpline at: 1-800-273-TALK.

Writing Emotion

Part of what led me to become a writer was that I didn't feel I could adequately express myself through normal conversations. Something was lacking. It took me time to learn to express myself clearly through writing. Writing about emotions can be tricky. The words, "I am angry," don't carry the weight of rage or show in any way the depth of emotion. We've become accustomed to using the shortcut language of words to convey what is very deeply felt. In the next exercises, you'll be asked to *express* your emotions in a clear and visceral way that is rooted in the body and how the emotions effect you physically. This can be cathartic, but it can also bring about intensely troubling emotions. If you find it's too much, take a break, and come back to this when you are ready. These exercises can be triggering, especially if you are writing about recent emotions.

WEEK 11: WRITING EMOTION

Body language is much clearer than words in conveying emotions. The scowl on a face clearly expresses anger or disgust. Stooped shoulders and tears convey sadness. It is much clearer to show rather than tell when discussing emotions, because we see emotions in other people and feel our own emotions in our body. For this exercise, practice conveying body language to show emotion. Pick four emotions (tired, scared, lonely, and angry, for example), and describe them through body language rather than words that signify emotions. You can write about yourself, and how you carry emotions in your body, or think of someone else you have seen in one of these states and describe their body language.

WEEK 12: WHAT'S IN YOUR HEART?

For this exercise you'll need colored pencils or pens, sequins and glitter, or other things you can use to decorate. Start by drawing the outline of a heart. Then think of all the things that make your heart happy. Inside the outline, draw and decorate or write down what brings joy to your heart. Think of words that bring you joy and write them down. Use the images and colors that come to mind when you think of the words and images.

Coping Strategies

Our bodies respond to extreme stress by triggering a "flight or fight" response where a flood of stress hormones called cortisol are released into the body, signaling the brain that it's time to either flee or stand your ground and fight. The hormones have several effects that help the body survive an attack: our heart rate increases, blood pressure rises, we begin to breathe faster. This dilates our blood vessels and the air passages in our lungs, which sends more oxygen to our vital organs and brain. Our senses sharpen. While under the duress of stress, we remain on high alert, and the reasoning and memory centers of our brains are less active, so our attention becomes more focused on either fighting the danger or running away from it.

If you're constantly in a stressful situation, with frightening or threatening situations occurring too frequently, stress becomes chronic and disrupts brain and body responses. High levels of stress have been linked to many different medical conditions like autoimmune disorders, high blood pressure, and mental illnesses. How do you know if you are under chronic stress?

There are a lot of things you can do to lighten the day-to-day stress of living in a racist society and help lower cortisol levels.

- **Connect.** Discuss emotional states with your parents; tell them how you are feeling. If your family is religious, see if there is a youth group at the church for your age group you can join. Spend time with your pets; pets are excellent for soothing anxiety and creating a calm connection. Dogs, for example, are proven to reduce anxiety in humans and that is why they can become great emotional support animals.
- **Practice healthy habits.** Drink plenty of fluids and eat a well-balanced diet; this will ensure that you are getting the

nutrients you need to stay physically healthy. Exercise too! Even just a brisk walk will help lower stress hormones and help stave off depressive episodes.

- **Tune out and unplug.** Take a break from the news and from social media and focus on the here and now. When kids witness catastrophic or violent events on the news, they sometimes get overwhelmed with feelings of powerlessness. Taking a break from media coverage can help. Instead, try to establish real connections by talking to your teachers, your friends, and your elders. They have great stories to share.

- **Engage in some hobbies.** Whether it's gardening or painting or coloring, hobbies also help with anxiety levels and give you something they can focus creative energy on. Journaling is an excellent way to process emotions and express some of the harder emotions you may not be ready to talk about. Keep your journal in a secure location. You can also explore your local hardware store classes and take up woodwork or coding if you like engineering. You can learn an instrument, as music is proven to be therapeutic and soothing. Photography is also a wonderful tool to help you focus on seeing the beauty around you, even in times of hurt.

- **Laugh it out.** Take time to find fun things to do, like watching a comedy on television—whatever will cause you to erupt in deep belly laughter. It may seem like it's impossible to laugh at some of the worst moments, but laughing is a great stress relief. Sitcoms, stand-up comedy, or even TikTok videos offer great comic relief opportunities for many of us. Alternatively: Scream it out. Go out into the backyard with a bucket of balls and let it all out, throw the balls as hard as you can, and scream at the top of your lungs. In a controlled setting, this can release a lot of pent-up anger.

- **Practice yoga and meditation.** Yoga increases flexibility and encourages calm and relaxation. There are also a number of deep breathing exercises you can practice, but try breathing in through your nose for a count of four, hold your breath for a count of seven, then exhale through pursed lips for a count of eight. In addition, you can use a guided meditation from one of the many available online or learn transcendental meditation as a family and practice it.

- **Go out.** Sometimes it can help to be out in the world in an environment where things are peaceful and relaxing. Go to a park and connect with nature. If you live near a beach or a lake, many people find that being near water is soothing.

- **Volunteer.** Ask your parents to join you and make it a family effort. While you can work for a cause geared toward racial justice, if you're having a hard time, you can also do something unrelated to racial justice, like volunteering at an animal shelter.

- **Try grounding exercises.** If you are stuck on a bad memory, try exercises to help focus on the here and now. Make it a game. Using all the senses, identify items in the environment you can interact with. For example, what three things can you hear? What three things do you smell, touch, taste, see? Use your senses to actually touch, taste, smell, see, and hear these things. If you are having an anxiety attack, counting exercises sometimes help to disable the panic. Count slowly to a hundred or a thousand. Coupling a counting exercise with walking works even better. Take a walk and count each step. This works by having the left side of the brain take over from the emotional center of the brain. It sometimes takes practice, so be patient.

- **Don't be afraid to seek out counseling.** The stigma related to getting help from a licensed professional often prevents Black people from seeking help they need. Talk to your parents about the importance of mental health counseling for you. Don't wait for a crisis to see a counselor; make it a weekly appointment. Don't give up if you don't click with your first therapist. It sometimes takes work to find a therapist who you feel comfortable with. Actress Taraji P. Henson has put together a resource guide to finding qualified Black therapists and virtual counseling groups for young adults and teens at her organization the Boris Lawrence Henson Foundation. You can find our more information here: borislhensonfoundation.org. Schools often offer counseling services, which is a good place to start for free.

WRITING PROMPTS:

Write Poetry and Create Art

Writing poetry and creating art are constructive ways of taking control over your emotions. They give you a tangible means of expression, allowing you to look closely at yourself and at a situation. They open you up to finding ways to cope with difficult situations.

WEEK 13: THE PANIC BOOK ACTIVITY

When you are filled with anxiety and panic, it's good to have something tangible you can pick up that will soothe your fears and help calm you down. The Panic Book Activity asks you to build a book of calming images and/or words you can open when you're feeling panicked and distressed. You'll need a blank sketchbook, coloring pencils and/or pens, and old magazines and photographs. You may also want to download some images from the internet with affirming quotes that will help steady you in times of crisis. Fill the book with sketches of things that soothe you, like the lyrics of your favorite song or pictures of a favorite pet. Keep the book handy for when you feel panicked and scroll through the pages, breathing deeply to relax yourself. The best time to work on this book is when your mood is calm, and you feel stable. But having it might help you with any moments of panic you experience in the future.

WEEK 14: RECOVERY POETRY

Along with being an author of nonfiction and fiction, I'm also a poet. Poetry is an excellent tool to use to uncover hidden emotions, play with language and sometimes just to have fun. In this week's writing prompt, we'll be using poetry as our medium for journaling. If you are new to poetry that can be a little intimidating. Just try to have fun with this exercise. Remember, no one has to see them if you don't want to show them to anyone, so you can feel free to write what you'd like.

For this poem, start by finding a word you believe should be in a poem. Let's say it's the color "red." Write "red" on a list. To complete the list, pick a word that begins with the last letter of the previous word. So in this case it might be "driver." Continue finding words that start with the last letter of the previous word until you have a list of ten or eleven words. Then, find a way to write a poem using each word in a line. For example, red would be in the first line, driver would be in the second line, and so on, until you have a ten or eleven-line poem.

Write in Nature

Getting out of the house, away from the electronics and reconnecting with nature can be a boost for your mood and can help you combat stress. There's nothing like that feeling of being part of something larger than yourself to refocus your energy and train of thought.

In our fast-paced world, it is easy to lose our connection with nature and forget that our very breaths are dependent on the health of the natural world. Reconnect with the life-giving source of a natural environment. First, find a place where you can be alone in a natural setting whether it is a forest or the beach or someplace with a hiking trail. If you opt for the hiking trail, take the path that's less traveled, even if it is steeper and rockier. Challenge yourself within reason. Wherever you choose to go, find a safe place there where you can settle in for some positive affirmations:

Today, I will spend some time in nature admiring its beauty and nurturing its health.

Today, I will respect Mother Earth by honoring her resources and treading lightly.

Today, I will be thankful for what the land provides to me and honor those who grow the food I eat.

Today, I will nourish seeds whether they are plants or ideas to make the world a better place.

Today I will protect all life whether it is plant, animal, or human, and treat it with care.

Today I will spend my time or resources on things that have positive impact on a global scale.

Today, I will focus on the plight of the hungry and envision a full plate for everyone. I will seek out guidance as to how to make my vision an actuality.

Think of this as a meditation. It will give you good practice in staying mindful and in the moment.

WRITING PROMPTS:

Meditation

Take out your journal and describe in detail your surroundings. Pay close attention to sensory images, sounds, how the wind feels on your body, any smells, and what you can see around you.

This writing exercise urges you to explore the outdoors and your inner wilderness. Nature can be cruel. The cycle of life and death is relentless. Forest fires, earthquakes, hurricanes, tornadoes—there are so many ways that nature seems to lash out at us. But it is also comforting to see rebirth and regrowth, and to know that the cycles continue even if we are not prepared to take our place in them. For this exercise, you'll be asked to write about what nature would say if it were to comfort you and offer you solace. It is helpful to actually be in a natural setting for this exercise, and it is most useful when you are experiencing grief or frustration over a crisis. Just take out your journal and imagine nature is speaking to you. Write down her wise words. You may find that the words work best as a poem. Whenever and however they come to you, write them down.

WEEK 16: MINDFUL DESCRIPTIVE WRITING

Mindful expressive writing can be a good source of meditation. To practice it, take five minutes and find something in nature and describe it in detail. If you're unable to go out, you can also focus on something in the room around you. Don't attach any thoughts or associations to your descriptions, no judgments, good or bad. Just describe the subject for five minutes.

Understanding Microaggressions

Microaggressions are daily interactions people of color and other marginalized groups of people have that rely on a bias or a stereotype and often leave the person of color feeling injured or angry emotionally. Sometimes these interactions are intentional, but often they are thoughtless comments and reflex actions.

Microaggressions wear me out. I've had to face plenty of them, from my work as a teacher to simply walking down the street. They are a daily part of life, and not something you get used to. It might be a white woman who touches a Black person's hair without permission just to satisfy her curiosity. It might be a white kid who uses the N-word because they think it's cool and have heard rappers use it. It's a complicated area that you'll need to understand to make sense of why it offends you. Even if they are minor, microaggressions can cause harm to people. At the very least, they can make you feel uncomfortable. Some of them will upset you.

Microaggressions never seem to stop. They come at you from everywhere, and they are difficult to respond to. The many different ways that a microaggression can sneak into your day are surprising, and they are often hard to recognize. Some of them are so subtle you find yourself asking if it was a microaggression at all or if you imagined it.

Microaggressions are made up of two parts:

1. The surface-level communication or words spoken (what the person actually says).
2. The unconscious meta-communication or the message that the microaggression delivers (how the microaggression is received by a Black person).

In this excerpt of his viral post about microaggressions, Brian Crooks tells the story of going to a friend's house in eighth grade to jump on his trampoline: "I didn't know the kid all that well, but we had some mutual friends and at that age, if a kid has a trampoline, you're going to jump on that trampoline. [...] We're jumping on the trampoline and [some] girls come out of their house and come over into his yard. Within about five minutes, they were laughing while saying, 'Get off our property, Black *boy*.' They'd clearly heard that phrase somewhere else before."

WRITING PROMPTS:

Your Life in Metaphors

Racism takes a physical and mental toll on Black girls. Metaphors are interesting (and often soothing) ways to view your life. They provide insight that literal thought cannot always provide. They can also help you reach your goals in an efficient, effective way. These next couple of exercises ask you to think in figurative ways to help you understand anxiety and your inner critic, and how to calm both when they are raging.

WEEK 17: THE PASSENGERS ON THE BUS METAPHOR

This exercise is designed to help you understand your thought processes and how your inner critic can make things more difficult for you when it is caustic and harping at you. Imagine you are the driver of a bus. The bus is a metaphor for your mind and the passengers are metaphors for your thoughts. Some of the passengers are quiet. Some of them are loud and critical, and some of them are kind and supportive. For this exercise, take your bus out for a ride and pick up passengers. Write in dialogue how the passengers react to the bus ride, and how you would respond to them in this situation. What happens when you hit a bump? How do you respond to overly critical passengers? What happens when the bus is full? How about when it's almost empty? How do the kind passengers make you feel? Take about ten minutes for this exercise.

WEEK 18: QUICKSAND ANXIETY METAPHOR

This exercise will help you see the futility of fighting an unchangeable situation. It is designed to help you think about alternative ways of dealing with anxiety and complicated situations. Imagine you are walking through a desert and step in a patch of quicksand and begin sinking into it. How would you react? Take a few minutes to imagine this scenario and then write about what would happen. How would it feel to fight to get out of the quicksand, only to sink further into it? Write about how it would feel to let go of any desire to escape the quicksand and let gravity take its course. How does it feel to struggle against a situation you cannot control? Write down all of your thoughts and the actions you would take to try to survive the quicksand.

Finding Sanctuary

The first step in dealing with microaggressions is to find a safe inner space—one you create in your imagination. When things get hectic or frustrating, and you need a quick way to relax and release stress, having a safe space in your mind to go to can work wonders for calming you down and clearing your mind.

To start, close your eyes and imagine the perfect sanctuary for you. If it's a place you already know, examine it closely in your mind for things you may have overlooked. Breathe deeply and let your senses experience the place and its surroundings. Make note of any people who share this space with you, and your feelings and emotions. Breathe in. Breathe out.

Finding a Safe Space

A place that feels like home can be a good place to conjure in your mind when things are at their worst and you need to chill out quick.

WEEK 19: HOMECOMING

In this exercise, you'll imagine a homecoming. Have you ever been to a place, or maybe it wasn't a place, but a situation where you met someone for the first time and felt like you had come home? Maybe it *was* your home. Whatever the case, you instantly felt at ease in your surroundings, and everything just felt right. Take a few minutes to imagine your homecoming and who greeted you when you felt at home and at ease. Try to figure out what it was about the place or situation that made you feel so comfortable. Imagine yourself feeling the same emotions you felt at the time. Then, take another ten to fifteen minutes to describe the place, the people in it and your feelings about being there. And remember, anytime you need to go to a happy place, all you have to do is close your eyes and focus on one of these two places.

WEEK 20: "GUEST HOUSE" POEM

The name of this exercise comes from the title of a poem by Rumi that speaks of the temporary nature of life and of emotions, both welcome and unwelcome:

"The Guest House" by Jalaluddin Rumi

> This being human is a guest house.
> Every morning a new arrival.

Begin by Googling and reading the poem, then answer some follow-up reflection questions designed to make you think about your emotions and how they visit you.

Reflection Questions:

1. What is your understanding of the poem?
2. Which emotions visit you most often? Why do they visit most frequently?
3. How might things be different if you welcomed all your emotions rather than rejecting some of them?
4. How can unpleasant emotions be beneficial?
5. How might you apply the message of "The Guest House" to your everyday life?

PART II: RECKONING

The Art of the Comeback

It can be difficult to know how to respond to a microaggression. You'll want to think about whether you want to respond at all, because people can get defensive when they are called out. Sometimes it just might be a bad idea to call someone out on their behavior, especially if the situation isn't safe for you to do so.

On page 78 to 93, I give you some tips on how to disarm microaggressions. It's a lot to take in, so remember that you don't have to read it all at once.

While it's a good idea to remain calm and patient with people who perpetrate microaggressions, it's also important to acknowledge how they make you feel. Remaining calm in the face of racist behavior will give you a sense of control, but don't make the mistake of denying your anger when you are belittled in any way. Your anger is justified, and if you use it creatively, it can make real changes.

Acknowledging Your Anger Is Part of Self-Care.

Self-care is the practice of tending to your emotional, spiritual, and physical well-being in a conscious manner. Practicing self-care can do things for you, like increase empathy, immunological response, and may lower anxiety and depression. Self-care has become a buzzword, but it's an important concept. The better we care for ourselves, the happier we are.

WRITING PROMPTS:

Remembering Self-Care

Fighting racism can wear you out. Make sure
you take the time to recharge and refocus your
energy. There are plenty of avenues to channel
your anger, like through art or writing. Racism
brings on complicated feelings, and journaling
helps you sort in all out, even in terms of your
own identity and behavior.

Remembering
Self-Care

WEEK 21: THE SELF-CARE BOX

In this exercise, you'll create a self-care box. Start by thinking about what self-care means to you. With your idea of self-care in mind, gather quotes and affirmations from magazines or online to line your box with. Decorate the outside of the box in colors that are comforting to you and place items like worry stones, photos, crystals, special pieces of jewelry, and anything else you think connects with self-care inside. You can even tuck away a gift certificate for a massage or your favorite coffee shop for when you're feeling run down. And fold up some quotes to place inside to peruse when you need a lift.

WEEK 22: EXTERNALIZATION

A problem can overtake your life if you overidentify with it and see it as a core part of your personality. For example, you might tell yourself, "I am useless" if you are unable to accomplish a goal you set, but you are not the problem. The problem is separate from you. You might have the problem, but it isn't who you are. In this exercise, you'll learn how to externalize a problem and see it as separate from your personality. Start by locating one of the things you tell yourself that is overidentifying with who you are as a person. For example, "I'm lazy" or "I'm stupid." Write down the problem statement. Next, look at the problem statement and pull it apart. What makes you lazy? What is it you failed to do that could change how you feel or think about yourself? Write that down too. Next, write down what you can do to make that statement hold less power. If it's "I'm lazy," for example, it might be washing your dishes or picking up your living area. Write that down too, but then follow up by doing the action statement you identified. Do the dishes. Pick up your living area.

HERE ARE SOME STRATEGIES FOR DEALING WITH COMMON MICROAGGRESSIONS.

While some of the tools given in the following section can be used to calm a frightening situation, let's be clear: we Black people don't have to constantly diffuse the fire. We must learn to validate Black anger, including our own, and express this anger. Sometimes being peaceful citizens works against speaking up for ourselves. Sometimes being polite simply doesn't work.

Words: "Don't blame me. I never owned slaves."
Why it's offensive: Suffering because of racism didn't stop when the slaves were freed. This statement denies any responsibility on the part of white people for the system of racism that still affects us today.
How to respond: Regardless of whether you personally owned slaves, white people continue to benefit from a system of racism that grants them many privileges. We all inherited a racist system from the forefathers of this nation. It is everyone's responsibility to create equal justice. When you say that you never owned slaves, it shows that you don't understand how hard it is for people like me to grow up with systemic racism, and you're belittling my experiences as a Black person.

Words: "White privilege doesn't exist."

Why it's offensive: It denies Black experiences with racism and implies that if there is no white privilege, then systemic racism is not a problem in society.

How to respond: You can grab a donut at 7-Eleven and while you walk around with it in your hand, looking at beverages, people still assume you are paying for your snack. That's a privilege that makes your life that much safer, one that a Black person like me doesn't have. In a racist system, people assume Black people are criminals and that white people will pay. The presumption that you have integrity as a white person is because of the color of your skin, not because of anything you did for your reputation. You did nothing as a white person to be presumed innocent except be born in a system that is racist.

And for the people saying, "not all whites are racist," know that you are *part* of a "racist" system. You participate in this system that perpetuates racism whether you are aware of it or not. And if you're white and this doesn't make sense, you need to do more work. Please do the work and get curious.

Words: "All lives matter."

Why it's offensive: We can see that Black lives do not matter in the news in stories like that of George Floyd, or Philando Castile, or Breonna Taylor.

How to respond: Brian Crooks explains perfectly why we say "Black Lives Matter." He writes, "When we say, 'Black Lives Matter,' [...] we aren't saying that *only* Black Lives Matter. We're saying, 'Black Lives Matter *too*.' For the entirety of the history of this country, Black lives have not mattered."

Words: "I'm not racist. I have a Black friend." | "I'm not a racist. I have several Black friends."

Why it's offensive: People have historically used the phrase to cover up racist behavior. Having a Black friend doesn't give you a "get out of racism free" card. It treats Black people as though they are a token object. We still see people try to defend insensitive or racist remarks by posting photos of themselves with Black people as if that immediately excuses their behavior.

How to respond: When you say, "I have Black friends" as an excuse to absolve you of your behavior, you are belittling the word "friendship." Black people are not monoliths, and there is no official Black seal of approval. Rather than leaning on your Black friendships to excuse your behavior, it would be more constructive if you thought of the ways your words and actions impact your Black friends and Black people you don't know all that well, and work to fight racism rather than engage in it.

Words: "Can I touch your hair?" | "Is that your real hair?"

Why it's offensive: There are several reasons asking to touch a Black person's hair is offensive, but the main reason is that it doesn't respect boundaries. In the same way you wouldn't ask a stranger if you could touch her breasts, it's just unacceptable to ask to touch a stranger's hair or ask questions about it. It also exoticizes Black hair and places the Black person in a position of being "othered." Black people report that people often touch their hair even without asking permission.

How to respond: When you ask if you can touch my hair, you seem to think I'm in a circus sideshow. I don't wear my hair this way for your amusement, and it is absolutely not okay to touch me in any way.

Brian Crooks tells of his own experiencing with having his hair touched: "From elementary school through middle school, I can't remember how many times the white kids asked if they could touch my hair. [...] I was a pretty shy kid. I was the only Black one, I was overweight, and I'd moved three times before I turned ten. So, rather than tell the white kids that no, they couldn't rummage through my hair, I just said yes and sat there quietly while they marveled at how my hair felt."

Words: "I'm color-blind." | "When I look at you, I don't see color." | "America is a melting pot." | "There is only one race, the human race."

Why it's offensive: Unless the perpetrator is blind or literally color-blind, they absolutely see color. What a person is saying when they say, "I don't see color" is that they are viewing the world through a position of privilege and can ignore injustices that are based on skin color.

How to respond: When you say, "I don't see color when I look at you," it shows you don't see me at all. I'm Black, and no amount of color-blindness is going to change that fact and what it means for me as a Black person. You can say something like that only because you are in a position of privilege where your own skin color doesn't affect you in the same ways mine does. Rather than not seeing my color, I wish you would look more closely at what it means to be Black and how it affects me, and people like me.

Words: "You are so articulate." | "You are pretty for a Black girl." | "You're not really Black." | "I don't think of you as Black." | "Why are you acting white?" | "You don't sound like other Black people."

Why it's offensive: Where do we start with this one? The problem with these microaggressions is that they single out an individual as superior to the rest of their race. "You're articulate" implies that most Black people cannot speak clearly and intelligently. "You're pretty for a Black girl" is straight up saying that most Black women are not attractive. These are all backhanded compliments. There is no one way a Black person looks or speaks or acts, so to point out the differences means that the perpetrator is saying, "you are different" while simultaneously insulting the rest of your race.

How to respond: When I hear you say [insert offensive phrase here], I'm not hearing that as a compliment. I'm hearing that you think other Black people are inarticulate (or ugly, or different, or stupid), and that's deeply insulting to me. Black people are all very different and to lump us all together into one group based on some people's traits is very demeaning and stereotypical. It tells me that you don't see people as individuals. You should get to know us better.

Words: "As a girl (woman), I know what you go through as a racial minority."

Why it's offensive: While sexism is a serious issue, the problem of racism affects people of all genders and the experiences are vastly different. In addition, Black women may have to deal with both the experiences of sexism and racism. Even if a white woman is sometimes discriminated against for her gender, she still has the privilege of being white.

How to respond: Sexism is a terrible problem, and I understand that it can be difficult, but the issue of racism is more complex than what you think, and even if you have had some bad experiences with sexism, you still have the privilege that comes with being white, so they are not the same thing. For example, if you are pulled over by the police, you can just hand over your license and registration and the matter is cleared up in a few minutes. For me, there is a lot more that goes into a police encounter. Black people are discriminated against in this society on every level, and that's not something you can understand simply because you are a girl (woman).

Words: "I believe the most qualified person should get the job." | "Everyone can succeed in this society, if they work hard enough."

Why it's offensive: Black people are far less likely to receive job offers even when they are as qualified as white applicants. Studies have shown that people with Black sounding names receive fewer callbacks, and that a white person with a criminal history is more likely to receive a call for a job than a Black person with no criminal history.

How to respond: Ideally the best qualified person would get the job, but if you do some research, you'll discover that there is a vast disparity in how many Black applicants get calls for jobs, even when their resumes show they are better qualified to do the work. When you say that, it belies the facts of the matter.

Words: (asking a Black person) "Why do you have to be so loud / animated? Just calm down." | "Why are you so angry?"

Why it's offensive: Historically, Black people have been told to be quiet, and are seen as violent if they express any anger at all. The subtle message being given is "sit down and shut up."

How to respond: When you say that, it tells me you don't understand how upsetting it is to be told to be quiet and settle down. I have a right to express my feelings on this issue. How would you like it if someone told you that you couldn't express your anger?

Words: Imitating accents or dialects.

Why it's offensive: Historically, Black people have been mocked for their accents and manner of speech in popular media and in minstrel shows. It's stereotyping and often done to make fun of a perceived lack of intelligence and to portray Blacks as thugs, idiots, or clowns.

How to respond: When you make fun of Black people by imitating their accents, you are perpetuating a harmful stereotype that doesn't show the diversity and intelligence of Black people. I find it offensive.

Words: "I'm not racist, but…"

Why it's offensive: A good deal of why this statement is offensive depends on what follows the "but." However, it is safe to assume that something racist is about to spill out of the perpetrator's mouth. The "but" is an attempt to make an exception to racist beliefs and to convince you that a little bit of racism is all right.

How to respond: I know you think you're not racist, but what you just said was very racist. We live in a racist society; it's impossible for you as a white person not to be even a little racist. Rather than qualifying your beliefs, why don't you do something to fight racism? You could call your local politicians, or join me at a protest, or support an organization that fights racism. Simply telling me you're not racist isn't good enough. Show me you're anti-racist."

Words: "Oh, you should meet my friend Devon. He's Black too."

Why it's offensive: This is similar to the "I have a Black friend" microaggression. It's offensive because it tokenizes a Black person, often to cover racist behavior.

How to respond: I'm sure Devon is a lovely person, but I'm wondering if you think I should meet him because we have something in common or because he's Black?

Words: Calling a Black woman or man "sister" or "brother," respectively. Or worse: "My nigga"

Why it's offensive: This microaggression is used to create a false feeling of allyship. It's offensive because it relies on stereotypical and sometimes offensive language.

How to respond: I'd prefer you not call me that. I find it offensive because it reinforces stereotypes. My name is_____. You can call me that.

These following last three examples are in the gray area that exists between microaggression and overt racism. Examples of this kind are prevalent in the day-to-day lives of Black people. In fact, in September of 2020, University of Michigan at Dearborn was heavily criticized for sponsoring a non-POC (people of color) Zoom event for white students to discuss racism. The issue with the event is that it didn't give Black students the opportunity to weigh in on issues that impact them directly.

Words: "Do you eat a lot of..."
Why it's offensive: It makes an assumption that all Black people eat the same thing and that there isn't a vast variety of cultures among Black people, and varied cuisines.
How to respond: When you ask me that question it makes me wonder if you are being racist or just plain ignorant. Black people eat all different kinds of foods, the same way white people do.

In this portion of his post, Brian Crooks writes about the pressure he felt being singled out: "My least favorite time of the year, every year, was February. Black History Month. Being the only Black kid in the class, I was the designated reader for the entire month. [...] Having an entire classroom of white kids stare at me while I explained what lynching and Black Codes were was pretty mortifying."

Words: "You people..."

Why it's offensive: It's a statement that marginalizes Black people and places them in an "other" category that is separate and unequal to the majority.

How to respond: When you say, "you people," I feel I am being disrespected for my color and cultural group and that is hurtful. Black people aren't just one monolithic group, we are vastly different individuals. If you took the time to meet and get to know us, you might be able to see us as individuals.

In this excerpt of his post, Brian Crooks talks more about the kind of racist incidents that shaped his life: "I was dating a girl when I went to college, and we broke up right before my sophomore year. She made sure to tell me she would never date someone outside of her race again when we broke up. As though A) I was the representative of all Black people, and B) I was going to have to explain to all Black men why she was unwilling to date them in the future."

Words: "But, but, but, what about Black-on-Black gun violence, huh?! What do you have to say about that?!"

Why it's offensive: Black people kill other Black people at about the same per capita rate as white people kill people of their own race. This argument is most often used to minimize the issue of police brutality. One thing has nothing to do with the other; violence among Blacks has nothing to do with police brutality or racial violence.

How to respond: Black communities have programs to fight the violence in their neighborhoods. This is a separate issue. I'd suggest you educate yourself about the rates of Black-on-Black violence if it's a topic that interests you, but I'm hearing you use it as an excuse for other violence, and that is unacceptable.

Speak up when you hear racist language or stereotyping or witness racist behavior. If it is not a safe situation, wait until it is safe. Look at racist encounters as an opportunity to practice speaking up for yourself.

Actions...And How to Respond

The type of microaggression known as a micro-assault can be the most difficult to deal with. Sometimes you'll find yourself questioning whether a microaggression just occurred because they can be very subtle. But sometimes they are so blatant you just can't believe one occurred and are at a loss as to what to do.

Here are some suggestions for dealing with micro-assaults and more flagrant acts of racism.

Action: Calling you the wrong (other Black person's) name: "Oh, sorry, wrong person!"

Message: "You all look alike" or "I can't be bothered to learn your name."

How to respond: Correct them. Say, "My name is _____."
If it's an ongoing problem, pull the person to the side and tell them, "I don't think you understand how much it bothers me that you haven't learned my name. I'd appreciate it if you'd stop calling me _____. My name is _____."

Action: Clutching their purse, dodging while passing a Black man or unnecessarily calling the police.

Message: Black people want to rob, rape, assault, or otherwise harm me.

How to respond: Depending on the situation, you might need to just back away; put your hands where they are visible and leave the scene. If the person is calling the police, you can say, "I have no intention of harming you. I'm leaving now." If the encounter escalates at all, pull out your cell phone and record the incident.

Action: A store owner following a customer of color around the store.

Message: Black people steal things from my store. They are suspicious.

How to respond: Your instinct might be to do your business elsewhere, but remember that in an equal world, you should be able to do business anywhere.

You have options:

- You can calmly confront the owner and use technology to document the interaction. If you don't capture the moment, or you wait until you get home to report the incident, chances are you won't be believed by Management or Headquarters; it's he said/she said at that point. It's a sad truth but, in this world, you need to learn how to document using video evidence.
- Another option is to ignore the situation and continue your shopping (while avoiding putting your hands in your pocket or purse). Then, check out of the store and leave. If you find it best not to confront a suspicious store owner or security guard as it could cause the situation to escalate, that's your choice—and yours alone—to make.

Action: Dismissing an individual who brings up race / culture in work / school setting.

Message: This is not an issue we feel comfortable discussing or, worse, there is no problem here.

How to respond: If you are the person being dismissed, take a deep breath, remain calm, and say:

> When you dismiss my concerns, it makes me feel like I'm not being heard. I know these issues can be difficult to talk about, but this is important to me.

And then continue with what you were trying to say before you were interrupted.

If it is someone else being dismissed, you can speak up and say:

> I'm interested in hearing what _____
> _____ has to say. Let's hear them out.

Action: Person of color mistaken for a service worker.

Message: People of color don't get better jobs than service positions.

How to respond: "I don't work here."

Action: Having a taxicab pass a person of color and pick up a white passenger or being ignored at a store counter as attention is given to the white customer behind you.

Message: The white customer has preferential treatment and should be waited on first.

How to respond: Speak up decisively. "Excuse me, I was waiting here." If the clerk doesn't respond, ask to speak to a manager. You can also contact the Better Business Bureau.

Action: A college or university with buildings that are all names after white heterosexual upper-class males.

Message: White upper-class heterosexual males are the only people who have contributed to the college's growth.

How to respond: Organize a protest and a petition drive to have some of the building names changed to reflect the diversity of the university. Contact the president of the university and let them know you feel the names should reflect a wider diversity of alumni.

Action: Television shows and movies that feature predominantly white people, without representation of people of color.

Message: Only white people are entertaining.

How to respond: Change the channel. Find programs with a diverse cast. Write the television station and let them know you would like more programs with people of color.

Action: Overcrowding of public schools in communities of color.
Message: Black children don't deserve the same kinds of facilities that non-Black children enjoy.
How to respond: Get involved with school board meetings. Petition the board to do a study for overcrowding. Contact your local politicians and write them letters about the overcrowding. Form a coalition of parents to address the issue with the school.

Microaggressions are painful.

Here, Brian Crooks explains the toll microaggressions (and overt racism) can take on a person of color: "I could tell you about the coworker who thought it was funny to adopt a stereotypical Black accent to apologize that we weren't going to have fried chicken and cornbread at our company Christmas party. I could tell you about the time I gave my floor mate a haircut freshman year and he 'thanked' me by saying he'd let a negro cut his hair any day of the week. [...] These are only a handful of the experiences I've had in my thirty-one years."

Problem Solving

Problems that seem to have no solution can become overwhelming and take on a life of their own. In the following exercises, we'll look at different techniques for finding solutions to problems, but one you can start with is to list your problems, then find three solutions for each. Out of the three, pick the best solution, and then solve your problem!

WEEK 23: MIND MAPPING

For this exercise, you'll be drawing a mind map to unsort a tangled problem. Start in the middle of a piece of paper and write down your problem. Circle it. Next draw lines coming off the problem, branching out from the center, and add different aspects to the problem. Keep going until you have a comprehensive overview of the problem and all of its aspects.

WEEK 24: STATEMENT OF POSITION MAP

A statement of position map lets you look at your problems and see how they are impacting different areas of your life. They are useful to you because you can clearly see how the problems affect you, and what core values these problems impact. To start this exercise, divide a sheet of paper into four columns. In column one, write down a list of your problems. In column two, write down what areas of your life the problem is impacting (home, school, work, relationships, etc.). In column three, evaluate the problem and how exactly it is affecting you in the different areas of your life. And finally, in column four, write down which of your core values is impacted by the problem. This should give you some motivation to solve your deepest issues, and an understanding of how far-reaching the impact of your problems is.

The Myth of Reverse Racism

We often hear from white people who claim that they have been discriminated against. They say things like: "You know what? I've been discriminated against, too. I experienced 'reverse racism' so don't talk to me about racism." Or "The way you talk about white people makes you a racist!" or "Why don't we have a White History Month?"

The problem with this argument is that it shows a lack of understanding about what racism is and how it operates. It comes down to the difference between systematic oppression and hurt feelings. White people can be discriminated against, yes. There are some bigots who hate all white people, yes, but it's not racism. The difference is that white people are in a position of privilege when it comes to race. We don't need a White History Month because every month is White History Month. One only needs to open up a history textbook to see which is the dominant culture. The equation is this:

Racism = oppression + power

Since coming to the United States through the Atlantic slave trade, Black people have never been in a position of power where they can oppress white people, so reverse racism is just a myth, just hurt feelings.

The Work of Becoming Known

Prompting a Reckoning

We tell stories to ourselves as a means of dealing with our lives. The way in which we tell these stories has a great deal to do with how successful and happy we are with our lives. Tell yourself a negative story: I'm never going to amount to anything because I'm poor, stupid, ugly, whatever you are saying to yourself, and you are pretty much guaranteeing yourself a negative outcome. Spin the story as a positive, or at least more realistic tale: It may be difficult, but I can do this, and you increase your chances of succeeding and finding lasting joy.

The next exercises ask you to reframe your narratives from negative ones into positive tales. To be clear, I'm not asking you to lie to yourself, just to be kind and tell yourself a truth that is easier to live with.

WEEK 25: BENEFIT FINDING, UNIQUE OUTCOMES

You may find this exercise to be emotionally difficult, and it can trigger negative thoughts and emotions, but it can also have some positive benefits if you give it a try. Resilience is built through seeing the positives even in negative situations, and this exercise will ask you to do that. First, think of an event that was traumatic or difficult and spend ten to fifteen minutes writing about it. Write down any emotions you felt or thoughts you have about the experience. Let yourself feel the emotions you felt during the incident. Next, focus on the positive outcomes of the experience and write about how going through this experience prepared you for other difficult challenges. What did you learn from the experience? How did things change for you as a result of this challenge in a way they would not have had you not experienced it?

WEEK 26: PROMPTING A RECKONING

Sometimes life gets to be overwhelming, and you can't contain all the thoughts racing through your mind. This exercise is especially good for sorting out your thoughts and calming your inner dialogue. To start, set a timer for fifteen minutes. At the top of a blank sheet of paper write, "This is what I think about and how it makes me feel."

Next, start writing all the thoughts that are racing through your mind including how they make you feel when you attach to those thoughts. After the fifteen minutes is up make a note of how you felt finishing the first part of the exercise. Next, go through your list and find the one thing that most irritates you or steals your joy. Circle that thought.

Lastly, create a fictional version of yourself. Someone who is you, but not quite you. She may be shorter or more athletic, but she comes close to being who you see yourself as. Write a story about her navigating the joy thief that you circled on your list from the free write. How does your fictional character reckon with the same problem you're experiencing? What can you learn from her? Spend a week working on this story for fifteen minutes a day, and then continue if the story isn't finished. You may find that you make peace with the nagging thought from your list, but you'll at least get ideas on how to navigate it better.

PART III:
VISUALIZATION

Living While Black

The sad truth is that being Black by itself is reason enough to expect that the police will be called. Black people are subject to having the police called on them for all manner of everyday, mundane activities like waiting for a business associate in a Starbucks and asking to use the restroom, babysitting non-Black children, having a backyard barbecue, not waving to a neighbor while leaving an Airbnb, or shopping while pregnant. Henry Louis Gates Jr. was arrested for "breaking into his own home" in Cambridge, Massachusetts near Harvard University's campus.

The prevalence of these types of stories has led to the founding of an organization called Living While Black that tracks and reports on instances where Black people going about their everyday routine find themselves handcuffed or questioned by police because someone found their mere presence suspicious. The number of stories from ordinary law-abiding Black people who've been suspected of criminal activity due to racial profiling is staggering.

There is no one good reason for this to happen, but some of the causes of unwarranted police calls have to do with how we live in the United States. Despite the repeal of Jim Crow laws, the US is still largely segregated by community and many white people have little to no contact with Black people in the course of their ordinary days; so simply seeing a Black person in a place where they are not accustomed to seeing them can send up a red flag. This is not to say that anyone's freedom to move should be limited in order to pacify anyone else's fears, but you should be aware of the phenomenon so you can be prepared to react in a way that will minimize the chances of a civilian or police encounter escalating to arrest or violence.

And this unwarranted harassment starts early, so it's important that you understand that as innocent as your actions may be, the color of your skin is enough to trigger a defensive reaction in some people, and you may find yourself facing a squad of police officers or an angry mob just because of your race. In the book *All American Boys* by Jason Reynolds and Brendan Kiely, Rashad's life is changed when a simple trip to purchase a bag of chips leads to him being beaten by a police officer who thinks he's shoplifting. What happens afterward polarizes his school and eventually the nation. If you are looking for a good book to read, I highly recommend it.

WRITING PROMPTS:

Be Free!

There are so many rules about living while Black
that sometimes it's helpful just to let go and be
free with your thoughts and expressions and not
worry about anything but writing. Sometimes
the best and most therapeutic writing comes
from letting go and writing whatever comes
to mind. In the next exercises, you'll practice
letting go of any inner criticism and writing what
occurs naturally. There can be a tendency to be
judgmental about our thoughts, but remember
we are not every random thought that crosses
our minds; we're much more complex than that.
Acknowledging your wayward thoughts and
feelings, even the most negative ones, often shifts
them into something new.

WEEK 27: FREE WRITE

For this first exercise just sit with a pen and a blank sheet of paper and write every wayward thought that comes to mind. It might look like this: "I have to schedule a hair appointment for next Tuesday, and do the dishes, and Sonia is coming to town next week I need to make arrangements to see her. Why does she always come during the busiest time of year for me? Oh, the dog was so cute earlier. I can't believe he fell into the pond…" Just let your stream of consciousness wander in whatever direction it wants to lead you. There's no set time for this exercise; see how far you get in twenty minutes. Remember to write everything down!

WEEK 28: SENTENCE STEMS

For this writing prompt, you'll complete a series of sentence stems. Write whatever comes to mind, but be thorough and detailed, and answer the "why" of each statement you make. Here are a few for you to try:

- I feel lonely when _____
- I have trouble sleeping when _____
- I worry most about _____
- I get angry when _____
- My happiest memory is _____
- My saddest memory is _____

Intersectionality

"Intersectionality" is a big word that is easy to understand once it is explained. It means that we all have a certain level of privilege, based on different factors in our life and that they combine in different ways to grant privilege differently to different people. For example, a Black woman is at a disadvantage both because she is Black and because she's a woman. She faces challenges both because she is subject to racism and because she is likely to experience sexism due to her gender. In another example, a white disabled man may have the privilege of being white and a man, but he faces challenges due to his disability; he won't face as many challenges as a Black man with disabilities, but he does not have the same advantages as an able-bodied white man.

There are a number of factors that combine in an intersection for every individual—some of these are an advantage, some a disadvantage—and we all experience intersectionality and personal power to varying degrees based on these factors. Some of these key factors include age, gender, economic status, ethnicity and culture, physical (dis)ability, education level, personal politics, religion, and sexual orientation. Understanding intersectionality helps people understand one another more clearly, and helps people find common ground.

Intersectionality is not a means to measure other people and make judgments based on how certain factors intersect, but it can be a useful tool in understanding how oppression works at differing levels based on a number of factors in addition to race. Understanding how intersectionality works can make it much easier to relate to other people who are different than you.

What can you do:

Listen: Pay attention to how people identify themselves and listen to what they have to say about their identities.

Recognize difference: Understand that different people experience the world differently. A person with a disability has a much different view of the world than a marathon runner, for example. Our differences can also be our strengths, and shifting your perspective to see the world through someone else's eyes can open your own eyes to different realities.

Avoid oversimplified language: Don't limit people to their identity labels. We are all much more complex than that.

Analyze the space you occupy: Do you hold space for others? Are you accommodating to people's different levels of need?

Seek other points of view: Try to be as broad-based and diverse in your interactions as possible. Meet a variety of different people and listen to their points of view. You may not always agree, but you may gain a better understanding.

Show up: Be there for people when they need someone. Hold a door for the man in the wheelchair who is struggling to exit the building. Be an ear to someone who needs you to listen to them.

Help someone to know how their varying identities may be experienced as helping or hurting themselves or others. But remember that some people don't want to learn about their own intersectional identities. Respect that and stop the conversation if they don't want to talk about it.

Oppressions, Violence, and Resistance are to a large extent determined by where a person falls on the identity wheel. For example, highly educated people may be more prone to doing anti-racist work, while an impoverished person may not have the resources to take the time out to lend a hand to the cause. Some people are more prone to being the victims of violent attacks—the elderly and infirm, for example.

The next few writing prompts take you into fairy tale and fable territory. I personally love fairy tales because they are filled with magic and intrigue. We can see intersectionality in fairy tales also. In fairy tales, the elderly, infirm and "othered" people and creatures play a big role in how the story pans out. See if you can write about intersectionality in these prompts about fairy tales.

WRITING PROMPTS:

The Story of Your Life

Fairy tales and fables are two of the ways we learn about life. Nearly everyone grows up hearing stories that have been passed down over generations. Applied to your own story, writing about yourself as a fairy-tale character can open your eyes to the magnitude of challenges you face and strengthen your resolve to keep fighting to achieve your goals. Try out these exercises for fun, but don't be surprised if you learn some valuable lessons about yourself in the process.

WEEK 29: WRITE AND ILLUSTRATE A FAIRY TALE ABOUT YOURSELF.

To start this exercise, imagine your "happily ever after" and what it will take you to achieve that kind of lasting happiness. Using whatever you have at hand write and illustrate your fairy-tale story. You can cast the antagonists/obstacles in your path as witches and dragons or trolls that you must conquer to find lasting joy. Don't make the mistake of thinking you have to be a helpless princess. Even Prince Charming needs a rescue every once in a while.

WEEK 30: UPDATE YOUR FABLE AFTER THE GLORY DAYS PASS.

Within the "happily ever after" that most fairy tales end with, there must have been continuing adventures. Rapunzel didn't escape her tower just to sit around looking pretty. If you have reached a stage in your life where you've reached many of your goals, it's time to update your fable and give yourself some new adventures. For this exercise, imagine yourself as queen of the castle. Write and/or illustrate a fable about your life now with all its continuing challenges. Imagine the next quest you must go on to achieve your goals. Slay some dragons.

Understanding Systemic Racism

What exactly is systemic racism? In short, it's a political system that follows policies designed to discriminate against one or more races of people. This discrimination can take many forms, but we typically think of it in terms of equal access to different services and programs, opportunity, and justice; it has become so embedded in our society that it's often hard to recognize as part of a system designed to make life more difficult for Black people.

Systemic racism is woven into the fabric of our lives, and the way it operates is similar to how we create habits. You can think of it in much the same way a person develops a fitness routine. Say you want to start a daily practice of running. For the first couple of weeks, it's difficult to get up in the morning, lace up your running shoes, and get out for a jog. Maybe you huff and puff and struggle to meet your goal; your running shoes aren't broken in at the beginning, and you find yourself sore and blistered at the end of the run, but over time, it becomes just another part of your daily routine; your body adjusts to the exercise. Your shoes get broken in, and you hardly feel the pain you felt at the beginning. Your feet develop calluses to protect you from the chafing your feet took in the beginning.

Systemic racism is like that. In the beginning, when it was being established, it was more overt than it is today. People were very direct about their intent to enslave thousands of Africans in the United States, but over time, it became just another part of the daily routine of life in the United States. To be clear, systemic racism is not the kind of overt racism you see in hooded Ku Klux Klan members or white supremacists; it's much sneakier than that, and not always easy to recognize. It's clear in the policies that charge Black people higher interest rates on home mortgages and car loans, and in the "school to prison pipeline" that doesn't give Black students a fair shot at leading a productive life.

Write a Letter to Yourself

Use your voice to change policies in your community. If you don't speak up and do something, who will? Attend town hall and city council meetings and speak if you have the opportunity. Start a blog about your community. Be vocal about the local, because it's often representative of larger systemic patterns.

Maybe you're still finding your voice, however, and you're wondering about ways to gain more self-awareness. Writing letters to yourself is an effective way of addressing issues you have but haven't been able to work on yet, either because of time or lack of motivation. No one knows you better than you know yourself, and no one else can be as forthright and blunt with you than you can be with yourself. It's important for you to be honest with yourself in these letters. You're also the best person to rally your own spiritual strength and bring yourself out of the blues after all. These next exercises are geared to get you communicating with yourself in an open, honest way. Bonus: You just might learn something about yourself that you weren't aware of along the way.

WEEK 31: WRITE A LETTER TO YOURSELF (FOR BAD DAYS).

This exercise in writing a letter to yourself is one you'll want to hang onto for rough days when it all just seems to be too much and you need a quick pick-me-up. We all have bad days, when it seems like the universe is conspiring against you and everything is just blue and cold. Those days when it feels like cracking a smile would take as much effort as running a marathon and you are just out of steam. This exercise asks you to write a letter to yourself for bad days to help boost your morale and see you through the dark times. First, wait until you are in an especially cheerful mood to write this letter. It doesn't make sense to write a cheerful letter when you're down in the dumps or not at your best.

Start by making a list of things that make you happy. Pick tiny, minute things like seeing a dandelion fluff blow into the wind or watching a small child learn how to walk. Write quickly and list ten things.

Then make a list of ten things you want to remind yourself of when you're sad. These might be people you can touch base with that are positive and have a tendency to cheer you up, or they might be things that always seem to soothe your nerves, like a hot cup of cocoa or a warm bath.

Then start writing your letter. Tell yourself that you love who you are (and why) and that we all hit rough spots where everything seems overwhelming and hopeless. In the letter, point out your positive qualities and remind yourself that bad times are temporary, even if they feel like they'll last forever. Give yourself some advice for seeing past the dark days that includes incorporating some of the items from your list of things that make you happy and things that soothe you. Remind yourself of times you thought you'd never find happiness again but somehow managed to crawl out of the dark spell. Encourage yourself to look on the bright side and see past the temporary doldrum. Suggest some self-care and let yourself know it's okay to feel blue; it's normal and part of living. Everyone has rough times, but they usually go away in a day or two. Sign it with love from yourself.

When you are done writing the letter, put it in a place where you can easily find it when you need it, and pull it out when you have a bout of depression or sadness or just one of those days where it seems nothing is going your way. Read the letter to yourself and be reminded it does get better.

WEEK 32: WRITE A LETTER TO YOUR FUTURE SELF.

This exercise is helpful if you are about to embark on a new venture with a new set of goals that you hope to achieve over time, like starting a four-year degree program at a college or university or starting a new job that you hope to advance in. You'll look forward to your future self and project into the future.

It is said that no one can ever enter the same river twice because the landscape and topography of a river is always shifting in sometimes imperceptible ways from moment to moment. We are all like rivers in that we all change in small ways from moment to moment and are never the exact same person twice. Think back to yourself ten years ago. You were vastly different than you are today, though the major parts of your personality and your physical embodiment may not have changed that much.

It's best to write this letter when you are having a good, happy day. To start, set a timeframe for your letter in the future. It can be one year, two years, four years or longer. Then think of all the goals you want to achieve in that timeframe. Write them down. Then, think of all the fears you have about achieving these goals or the personal fears you carry. Maybe you're afraid of public speaking and want to become more self-confident in front of a crowd. Write those down as well.

Next, draft the letter to yourself looking into the future when you have achieved all the goals you've set for yourself and maybe failed at meeting a couple of them. Tell yourself how proud you are of facing your fears and meeting your goals, and that it's okay if you haven't met everything you set out to do. Imagine how it will feel once you have put your fears aside and conquered them. You can also anticipate the new anxieties you'll be facing at the end of this timeframe and let yourself know you have faith you'll conquer those, too.

When you are done writing the letter, sign it with love and seal it up in an envelope. If you want, you can include some photos of you as you look right now to remind yourself of who you were when you wrote the letter. Write "Do Not Open Until [Date]" on the outside of the envelope, and then either place the letter in a prominent place where you'll see it often and be reminded of your goals or put it away for safekeeping. When the timeframe passes, reread the letter, and maybe write a new letter to another future self.

Never Argue
with an Idiot

No matter how vocal and active you are, there are just some people who will never accept that systemic racism and implicit bias are issues in this day and age. You can run yourself ragged trying to convince a bigot that he or she is bigoted, and the only thing that will accomplish is that you'll wear yourself out fighting a losing battle. It's not your job to convince the world that Black lives matter. Some people cannot be swayed no matter how persuasive the arguments you provide them.

Rather than providing racists with research, point them in the right direction and let them research the issue themselves. If they aren't willing to put in the legwork to educate themselves, they simply aren't interested in learning. There is only so much you can do with people who are willfully ignorant.

Do answer questions. People are capable of change, but they need to show a willingness to learn. It may be awkward for them at first. Be patient, but suggest they talk to other people of color so you aren't alone in trying to sway someone. A person is more likely to see the other side if they have more than one resource to rely on. Suggest that they step out of their comfort zone and just listen to what is being said.

But put your energy toward community alliances and group efforts. It's okay not to win every debate.

WRITING PROMPTS:

Talk It Out

It's important to spend time with those we don't always agree with. Otherwise, we end up telling ourselves that they don't matter. Our need to reach out to others gradually disappears until it becomes almost unthinkable to be with them.

Dialogue, the interaction between characters, is a driving force behind plot and reveals character in fiction and it can work that way in real life as well. In a practical sense, writing dialogue can help you by opening you up to imagined conversations you might dread having in real life. You might surprise yourself by finding that the conversations you worry about aren't that difficult if you write them down first as practice.

WEEK 33: DIALOGUE

There are several approaches you can take to this exercise. The first one is to write the conversation you dread having in real life—like a first-time conversation with an estranged parent, a confrontation with a bully, the dialogue from an encounter with authority, etc. Just imagine what would happen if you opened up and let it all out with another person you've been wanting to talk to but have been avoiding because you're afraid it might be awkward. Write their responses as you imagine them happening. Pay attention to imagined body language. How would the person respond to you? The other approach you can take to this exercise is to have a dialogue with another part of yourself. For example, you can write a dialogue between your past self and your future self. Or have a conversation with your awkward teenage self.

WEEK 34: WRITE A LETTER TO YOURSELF (FROM SOMEONE ELSE).

You may consider mentioning how the power of forgiveness is rarely for the person whom we forgive but for ourselves.

In this exercise, you'll be giving yourself the gift of a letter you wish someone close to you would send. Think of someone in your life with whom you have some stored anger, resentment, or pain. Someone who's wronged you in some way and hasn't made an attempt to reconcile or apologize for their behavior. Find a period of undisturbed time and focus on this person and the feelings your interaction with them has triggered in you. Spend some time thinking about what you wish they could tell you to make the situation right again. What would it take for you to forgive them and for those feelings you're holding onto to dissolve?

Then take on the other person's voice and persona and write yourself a letter saying all the things you wish you could hear from them. Really put yourself in the other person's shoes and try to see things from their perspective. Write from that perspective and include any emotions you think they may be harboring toward you. Allow yourself to forgive any mistakes you may have made in the encounter like overreacting or lashing out in anger.

You may find this exercise is cathartic and loosens up emotions you've been clinging to tightly. It isn't unusual to find yourself crying after signing off the letter. You may also find the exercise raises feelings of compassion toward the other person. You may find yourself forgiving them for their shortcomings and having a better understanding of what led to your falling out. Whatever the letter-writing triggers in you, take some time when you are done writing it to release any stored emotions. Take some deep breaths and focus on forgiving the other person. The power of forgiveness is rarely for the person whom we forgive, but for ourselves.

Some people like to burn the letter after they've written it to ceremonially put the matter to rest. You can do this, or throw it out, or store it in a safe place where you can revisit it the next time you have a falling out with this person. You may choose to write a letter to this person about the grievances you have with them, and in the letter apologize for your part in the matter. You may choose not to forgive them if the argument was heated or if you aren't ready for forgiveness. Whatever you choose to do, the important thing is to try to understand the other person's side of the argument and find some peace.

Racial Profiling and Police Encounters

Darren Martin, a former White House Staffer under President Obama, just wanted to move into his new home. While in the process of doing just that, he found himself surrounded by half a dozen New York City policemen who were under the impression he might be armed and dangerous. One of his new neighbors had seen him moving in, and assumed he was an armed burglar. "It could have been the TV, the couch, the pillows—I don't know," Martin said. "It's a fear of Black men that makes people see things."

The problem of racial profiling is one that affects many people of color, even non-Blacks. And it's a much broader issue than just increased police calls about suspicious activity. Think of a post 9/11 world, where travelers of Middle Eastern descent are subject to "no fly" lists and more thorough TSA screening at airports, or of anti-immigrant sentiments that lead to increased immigration raids in areas with high Latinx populations.

The phrase coined to describe this kind of behavior is "implicit bias" and it has a broad ripple effect. It starts with ideas developed during childhood and ends with more police calls and arrests for Black and other minority citizens than for whites. Racial profiling in law enforcement isn't good for anyone. It bogs down police departments with unnecessary calls and can create a division between police and the communities they are sworn to serve and protect.

The statistics for Black people and law enforcement are alarming when placed in comparison to those of white people. Black people are subject to more traffic stops. They are more likely than whites to be shot and killed when unarmed. They are more likely to be handcuffed and detained without arrest, pepper sprayed or pushed to the ground compared to whites, and more likely than whites to be searched.

It's important to prepare yourself for the likelihood that you will be stopped by police, because no matter how law-abiding you are, there's a good chance you'll have to cope with the police at some point.

Rules may vary from one state to another, but there are generally three types of typical police encounters:

Consensual Encounter. During this kind of police encounter, the officer initiates a conversation that doesn't involve any show of force like police sirens or orders. You are free to leave and have the right not to answer any questions or identify yourself.

Investigatory Detention. During this kind of stop, there is reasonable suspicion of criminal activity. The person being detained must identify themselves. You do have a Fifth Amendment right to remain silent during an investigatory stop.

The officer stopping you usually has the right to perform a brief frisk for weapons (check the rules for your state), and if one is located, may perform a full search. You still have the right to refuse a full search, but the officer may do this against your will (again, check the rules as they apply to your state). You do not have the right to walk away during an investigatory stop. Probable cause that a crime has been or is about to be committed must exist for an investigatory stop to take place.

Arrest. In order for an arrest to occur, there must be probable cause to believe you have committed a crime. In an arrest, physical force or authority is used to prevent you from leaving, and typically a person is placed in handcuffs. You have your Fifth Amendment right to remain silent during an arrest, but you must cooperate with the police. You do not have the right to leave.

Police are supposed to protect us from danger and guard us. If you ask small children to point out a hero, many still designate a police officer. It is unfortunate that the number of fatal police encounters has created a situation where they are justifiably feared by many people in the Black community. Knowing your rights during a police encounter can do a lot to help ease your anxiety. Next, we'll look at your own heroes from childhood and ask you to write about them.

WRITING PROMPTS:

Childhood Dreams and Heroes

Your very existence defies history. Never forget those who broke the unjust rules society once used to limit their progress, those who fought hard to get you to this moment, those who gave light so others could find the way through dark times. Because of them, you get to walk into a restaurant through the front door, sit at the front of the bus, and cast a vote for leaders who represent your ideals. Walk in the freedom they secured for your sake. Be proud of your rich skin, and may your hair be a crown that stands tall. Be proud of your deep-rooted culture(s). Be proud of the power of those who came before you, as the strength of generations will propel you forward and carry you through difficulties.

As you fight racism, think about the legacy you'll leave—whose hero will you be?

WEEK 35: CHILDHOOD DREAMS AND HEROES

We all have childhood dreams and heroes—people we looked up to as children and continue to admire as adults. These are people who inspire us in many different ways. Maybe it's Beyonce for her creativity and talent, or your grandmother who, despite unforgiving circumstances, always seems to prevail. In these exercises, you'll look at some of your heroes and discover your own superpowers. Your heroes and heroines, whomever they may be, tell you a lot about yourself. For example, if you admire Harriet Tubman for her tenacity and willingness to risk her life for the freedom of others, you may have the same kind of bravery. Spend ten minutes writing down the names of the people you admire, then write down the traits that make you admire them. Go a little deeper than just admiring someone for beauty or glamour—write about the core qualities and beliefs they possess that you admire. Then, ask yourself which of these qualities you possess and which you'd like to develop.

WEEK 36: MY SUPERHERO CAPE

I've met many people I consider to be superheroes. They are just ordinary people who seem to be extraordinary. A superhero or superheroine doesn't have to be someone who wears a cape, but in this exercise, you'll be asked to think of admirable qualities as superpowers. First, draw the outline of a superhero cape. Next, think of a person you admire greatly—someone who is an ordinary person you know personally. Write their admirable traits on the outline of your superhero cape. Maybe they are unusually thoughtful or fun. Maybe they are committed or resourceful. Whatever qualities you admire in them write on the cape. Now, write about how those qualities make them resilient and able to overcome hardships. Which of these qualities do you possess? How do they make you resilient? Write about that, too.

Your Rights During a Police Encounter

Remember that you have rights during a police encounter. Please check whether these apply to your state, but these are your common rights:

You have the right to remain silent. You may be required to identify yourself, but you have the right to indicate you do not wish to speak with the police or answer any questions (Google "Miranda Rights"). You do not have to answer any questions about where you were born, how you entered the country or your immigration status in most police encounters, though this may be different in an airport or at a border crossing.

You have the right to an attorney. You can refuse to answer any questions without legal counsel. You may have the right to have an attorney provided for you if you are arrested and cannot afford an attorney.

You have the right to refuse to be searched. A police officer can pat you down for weapons, and may conduct a search without your consent, but it will be noted if the search was consensual or not.

Know your rights! It's fine to give your name to an officer, but once the questions go beyond that, you should immediately ask for a lawyer.

A portion of Brian Crooks' story on social media relates a harrowing police encounter just up the street from his parents' home in Naperville, Illinois. Once, when Brian Crooks went home on a visit from college, he was pulled over less than a block from his parents' home. It was a late winter night, around midnight, and it had snowed that day, so Brian wasn't speeding. He hadn't been drinking either. The police officer had his gun drawn when he stepped out of the cruiser. He told Brian to drop his keys out the window, and to exit his car with his hands up and step backward toward him slowly. Brian knew the police officer was off base, but he also knew that any failure to comply might be interpreted as an act of aggression. He didn't want to be shot to death—particularly not down the street from his parents' house. So he did as he was told.

The policeman handcuffed and frisked him, and Brian spent about fifteen minutes handcuffed in the cold while the officer searched his car. The officer refused to explain why Brian had been pulled over, or why he was being detained. It was only when Brian was secured in the back of the squad car that the officer explained there had been reports of gang activity in the area, and that a car and driver that matched his description was involved in said gang activity. Gang activity in south Naperville didn't sound likely—and neither did the idea that it was committed by a Black male driving a flashy blue Mazda MX-6 with a showy blue and white interior.

The policeman was very short when he asked what Brian was doing in that neighborhood so late at night. When Brian explained that his parents lived at "the house with the glass basketball backboard just over there," the policeman didn't believe him. He had Brian exit the squad car once again and placed him face down on the hood to frisk him one more time. Brian's identification listed his parents' address, but the policeman still didn't believe that he lived in that house. Brian thought the policeman might accuse him of having a fake license. It was only after about a half hour when his record was cleared, his car was searched for the third time, and nothing was found that the policeman let Brian go reluctantly.

The policeman didn't apologize, or admit his mistake, and of course he wouldn't acknowledge that he'd lied about a Black gang leader in south Naperville driving a gaudy blue Mazda MX-6. The officer watched from his squad car as Brian drove to his parents' house and stayed outside in the street as Brian opened the garage door, parked his car inside, and then shut the garage door.

Remembering Who You Are

Say it:

- I am Black and I am proud of my identity.
- I keep my self-control around people who question my history and my identity.
- I protect myself from people who question my values and my culture.
- I realize with wisdom and discernment the discrimination that my community encounters.
- The strength of my ancestors is so bright, that it becomes more than enough.

Forgive yourself for feeling anger, hatred, or contempt for people who see you as an inferior being. Take a deep breath. You'll need some supplies for the next few activities including thick cardboard as a base for your collages, old magazines, newspapers, or picture books, scissors, and glue, plus anything else you'd like to decorate your collage with.

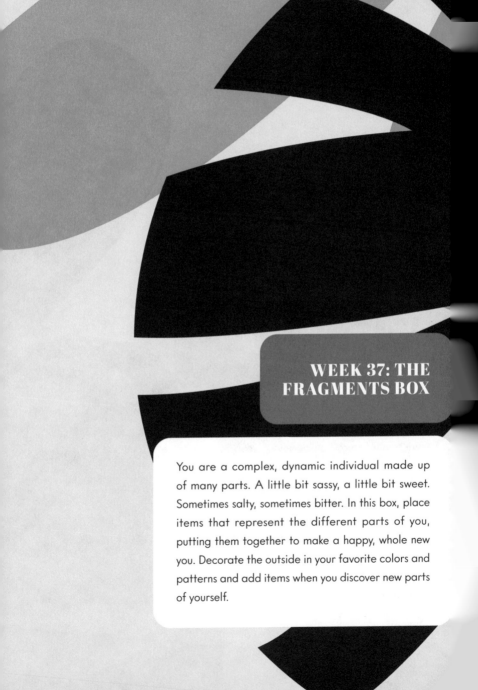

WEEK 37: THE FRAGMENTS BOX

You are a complex, dynamic individual made up of many parts. A little bit sassy, a little bit sweet. Sometimes salty, sometimes bitter. In this box, place items that represent the different parts of you, putting them together to make a happy, whole new you. Decorate the outside in your favorite colors and patterns and add items when you discover new parts of yourself.

WEEK 38: "WORDS TO LIVE BY" COLLAGE

Having a visual reminder of your core values can help you remain focused on achieving your goals. Take a couple of minutes to think about your core values and what's most important to you in life. You can jot down a list of words or phrases to help guide you during the next step of this exercise. Then, cut out words and images that represent these words from old magazines and newspapers and paste them to a piece of cardboard in a collage. Hang the collage somewhere you'll see it every day.

How to Stay Safe During a Police Encounter

We most often hear about Black men facing police encounters, but it's an issue for Black women, too. Breonna Taylor and Sandra Bland both died after police encounters. If you are pulled over or stopped by a police person, make sure you know how to stay safe and document everything that happened when it's safe to do so.

- Remain calm.
- Keep your hands visible at all times.
- Be polite and cooperative, but do protect your rights.
- Don't run, resist, or obstruct the police.
- Don't lie or provide false documentation.
- Keep your vehicle in good operating condition.
- Make sure you have your paperwork handy.
- Don't argue with the police.
- Turn off the ignition in your vehicle.
- Explain where your paperwork is before reaching for it.
- Ask the officer to turn on his body camera.
- If you feel unsafe, call 911 and ask the dispatcher to send a Sergeant or Lieutenant to assist you.

Nowadays, it is also easy to turn on your cellphone camera and record what's happening, but do so only if it's safe.

WRITING PROMPTS:

Journal with Photographs

As a Black girl, you may become overwhelmed by the pictures you see in the news—many portraying violence against people of color. In the following prompts, you will use pictures that inspire good feelings instead.

Photographs are excellent journal tools because they evoke emotions and can instantly transport you to a different place or time. You can reconnect with people you no longer see or have lost to death or other estrangements. There are many different ways of using photographs as a tool for journaling. These next two exercises offer a couple of options for you to try out.

WEEK 39: JOURNALING WITH PHOTOGRAPHS

Find a photograph or a group of similar photographs. It's even better if there are other people in the photograph with you, but it can be a single person. Start by remembering when and where the photograph was taken, and then delve deeper into the story behind the picture. What just happened? What was about to happen? How do/does the people/person in the photograph feel? How is that different than how they look? What are your thoughts and feelings about the photograph?

WEEK 40: TIMED JOURNAL ENTRIES

This next exercise is good for you if you have trouble focusing your thoughts. Think of something you've been having trouble focusing on lately, find a photograph/image that represents it, and then set a timer for five to ten minutes and write only about that topic. You'll feel yourself want to slip into other subjects, but really restrict yourself and focus on the one topic. You can do this anytime you have trouble focusing on something.

How to Fight Systemic Racism

It's important for everyone, regardless of race, to ask, "What is my role in this system?" and then do everything possible to dismantle it, starting within ourselves.

How to Fight Systemic Racism

- **Test yourself!** I suggested earlier in this book taking one of the implicit bias tests created by a consortium of scholars at the University of Washington, Harvard University, and the University of Virginia. These tests—there are several—measure your unconscious bias toward other people of different races, ethnicities, and religions. You may discover that you have some hidden biases of your own to be mindful of. The tests can be found at implicit.harvard.edu/implicit/takeatest.html.
- **Speak up!** If you see (or are the victim of) overt racism and it is safe to do so, say something. Challenge racist behavior (but, again, only when it's safe to do so).
- **Defend democracy.** Attend protests and town hall meetings where racism is a central concern. If you can afford to, support local and regional bail bond funds that help provide legal assistance to demonstrators who are arrested while exercising their civil rights.
- **Learn anti-Black history.** There are a number of documentaries and podcasts available for you to watch and listen to, including Ava DuVernay's documentary 13th, available on Netflix. Or listen and read The 1619 Project, available on the web. (The project has become controversial, and the controversy itself is quite fascinating.) Knowing

about the early days of systemic racism in this country will help you put in context what is happening today.

- **Know your rights and defend them.** Check out the ACLU, the Southern Poverty Law Center, and other organizations that work to protect civil liberties. Demand action by contacting your local leaders, but don't stop there. Contact your representatives in Congress and the Senate. Sign petitions. Vote with your conscience.
- **Challenge the notion of color-blindness.** Color-blindness actually makes racism worse, because it rests on the supposition that all races are treated equally. While it may be true that we are all equal, we are not treated equally, and color-blindness just creates an excuse for people to overlook inequity when it's apparent.
- **Put your money where your mouth is.** Join the boycott of companies that don't actively fight for equal justice. Spend your money at Black-owned businesses, and, if you can, support organizations that work to fight systemic racism.
- **Know your values, and act accordingly.** Stick up for those who are being bullied, for example. Find out what other people value and surround yourself with those who share the same values as you. As you'll read in the next prompt, values can change over time, so look for people willing to change themselves; they may become an ally in your fight against systemic racism.

Visualization

In these exercises, you'll look forward in time and visualize the future you'd like to lead.

Think of a problem you currently have and close your eyes and imagine yourself as you would be in five to ten years if you do not solve the problem. Write what your life would be like. The second method is to think of yourself problem-free in five to ten years and write about what your future would hold without any major problems. Where would you be? Who would you be?

WEEK 42: HOW DID THE CHARACTER CHANGE?

Our fictional heroes and heroines evolve. It's one of the reasons we get attached to them. We like to see the wicked mend their evil ways and become good, or for the weak to become strong; we want to see the joyless person find and maintain some happiness in their lives. It's difficult to remain interested in someone who is static and never changes at all. And fact follows fiction. This applies to real life as well. Facing and overcoming obstacles in life leads us to making new discoveries about ourselves and learning lessons, which changes who we are on a fundamental level. Think back to when you were in second grade. You are a much different person now than you were then because you've learned and have grown. Change is a little like trying on new clothing. You see what fits, try things on and put back what doesn't suit you. For this exercise, think back to the last time you made a big change in your life and write about how you were altered by the experience. Write for about ten minutes, noting all the details of the change. Next, think about a change you'd like to make. It can be something big or something minor, but you have to believe that you are capable of making the change happen. Write about the things holding you back from making the change. How can you overcome those obstacles? How will your life be better if you make the changes you want?

PART IV: IMAGINATION

Using Creativity and Self-Confidence Against Racism

Nurturing your creativity and self-confidence will go a long way in helping you deal with racism. Being creative will give you an outlet for some of the anger you are likely to feel at being discriminated against, and being creative helps in many different ways. It will help you learn creative ways of sticking up for yourself, for example. In this chapter, we'll talk about different ways you can be creative, why it's important, and how you can encourage others to develop self-confidence.

Support your creativity. Having a creative outlet will help you through difficult times. Without a creative outlet, our emotions get pent up and that can lead to mental health issues down the road. It's best to find creative ways to express yourself so that you have the strength and confidence to deal with racial injustice that will likely occur over the course of your life.

Creative thinking and creative problem solving go hand in hand. If you feel free to express yourself, you will spend less time internalizing negative messages you receive from elsewhere and more time focusing on growth in the areas that are important building blocks to a happy life. Becoming a creative person doesn't just occur naturally—it requires nurturing and patience. Here are some tips to help you explore your creative side:

Gather the tools you'll need. You want a wide variety of media to engage in self-expression. Things like crayons, finger paint, and colored pencils are a good start, but think outside the box, too. Go to the craft store and explore different arts and crafts. See what you'd like to try out and spend a little bit of money each month gathering supplies. Don't get discouraged if you don't like all the things you try; you probably won't like them all, but trying them out is a good way to find what fits best for you. Do an internet search for Black artists like Jacob Lawrence, Romare Bearden, Elizabeth Catlett, or Faith Ringgold. Contemporary artists like Kehinde Wiley also play an important part in depicting Black history through art, and the creativity they display can connect you to Black culture. Getting to know Black artists can help you see the long history of Black art and culture.

Designate an area in your home for creative expression. Make your home a laboratory for creativity. A special area designated for creativity will help keep down the mess that often comes with creative expression. Decorate the area with your own art, but also that of Black artists you admire.

Read for fun and participate in the arts. While for many years it could be challenging to find books that (positively) featured Black characters, there has fortunately been a large increase in the number of "diverse" books published in recent years—books that build confidence and instill pride in young Black readers, and counter negative messages that you may be hearing from other media outlets. If there is an active arts scene in your area, try attending different arts events, especially if they feature Black artists or writers. Explore modern Black music, or plan some time to watch powerful Black films and discover Black filmmakers like Issa Rae, who became the first Black woman to create and star in a premium cable series (she is the creator and star of HBO's hit series, *Insecure*), or Ava DuVernay who became the first Black woman to direct a film nominated for a Best Picture Oscar (*Selma*) and is also the first Black female director to win the director's prize at the Sundance Film Festival in 2012.

In his *Time* magazine essay, *The Renaissance is Black*, author Ibram X. Kendi links the idea of Black Renaissance as stirring Black people to be themselves and lists the Black creatives who make this possible. It is a moving and powerful read. Appreciating and understanding Black literature and Black art will not only give you a rich art education, but it will also help you understand Black culture, Black history, and the serious race and social justice issues Black people are facing right now.

Keep it simple. Especially in the beginning, there's no need to spend a lot of money on creative supplies. Not everyone can afford a grand piano, but an electronic keyboard may be within reach. For visual arts, you can recycle brown paper bags into a canvas for coloring or painting, for example. You can use torn paper bags to make collages, or collage with magazine photos. There are many ways to express yourself artistically that don't cost a lot of money.

Do something creative every day. Be creative in your thinking about what creativity is exactly and make it part of your day, whether it is journaling or listening to music or something completely different.

Being creative can be as simple as making yams and collard greens. It's a physical experience that ties you to the culture of Africa, and something you can enjoy. Braiding hair is another example of an activity that ties you to your culture and can be done frequently and with creativity. Whatever it is, make it part of your everyday life.

Find and pursue your passions. Pay close attention to what comes naturally to you and makes you happy, whether it's writing or painting or playing a musical instrument or something else entirely; dancing or rapping can become an outlet for confidence and fighting prejudice, and you can easily channel a talent for painting into an education about Black artists. But be careful:

Don't care so much about what you achieve. You don't have to be the best at everything you do. Try and fail and try again or try something else entirely. Learning to lose gracefully is an important lesson.

Creativity isn't just about arts and crafts. It's a way of life. There are several benefits to engaging in creativity. It leads to creative problem solving, reduces stress and anxiety, encourages innovation, and leads to feelings of pride and accomplishment, to name just a few of the many ways creativity is good for you. Besides those, it's just plain fun.

WRITING PROMPTS:

Make a Collage

Art therapy, collage in particular, is a beneficial exercise that can help you improve motor function, boost self-esteem, reduce conflicts with other people and much more. It also gives you a nonverbal means of expressing emotions through a visual medium. You'll need some supplies for the next few activities including thick cardboard as a base for your collages, old magazines, newspapers, or picture books, scissors and glue, plus anything else you'd like to decorate your collage with.

WEEK 43: CREATE A COLLAGE OF YOUR WORRIES.

We all have worries and nagging doubts, but sometimes they can be overwhelming. This next exercise will give you a book you can turn to when panic and anxiety get out of control. First, make a list of things that worry or trouble you in your day-to-day life and then search through old magazines for images that represent these worries and fears. Paste them to a piece of cardboard. As you are cutting out the images, focus on taking the power back from the worries so they have less control over you. It may be easier to face them if you have a visual representation of them to look at.

WEEK 44: DESIGN A BOX.

Designing a box is fun, but it also gives you a place to tuck away little treasures. Dedicating boxes to specific items is a good way to remind yourself that you're worthy and special and unique. In this week's exercise, you'll design a few boxes to remind you of who you are, how to take care of yourself, and what's important to you. You can find inexpensive plain wooden boxes at the craft store or recycle cardboard boxes to suit your needs. You'll need paint, glitter, sequins, lace—anything you want to decorate the box with. You can even clip out words or photos from magazines and use some Mod Podge to seal them. The biggest part of designing these boxes is to let your imagination run wild.

Self-Esteem and Confidence

I find that boosting other people's self-esteem is a good way to keep my own in check. If my self-esteem is lagging, often it just takes a good talk with a friend going through some of the same struggles to put my mind at ease and feel better about myself. Some other things you can do to inspire self-confidence in yourself and in your friends:

- Read positive and affirming books and watch positive and affirming programming with your friends and family.
- Let your friends hear you say kind things to other people.
- Start listening to what your friends are saying about themselves and correct them if you hear negative self-talk. If, for example they say, "I'm stupid," ask them why they would say such a thing. Oftentimes it's just frustration over something they are struggling with.
- Praise your friends' efforts, not just the end results.
- Send your friends notes and let them know they make you proud. Maybe not every day, but once in a while, surprise them by letting them know you think they are talented, strong, and smart.
- Learn about personal affirmations for when you go through a bout of self-doubt or self-pity—phrases like: "I am strong," "I am unique," and "I can make a difference."
- Learn about role models from history and trailblazers you can look up to and be inspired by, and share these with your friends.
- Find role models you can look up to and spend time with them.

Building self-esteem is an ongoing process. It can take years and years of hard work to maintain and build self-confidence. Try your best to always remember you are your own best friend, and that there's no one quite like you in the world. There's no one better than you on the planet. There's no one worse either. If you work hard at building your self-confidence, it will make the messages you receive from elsewhere in the world less important, because you will trust your own judgment of yourself.

WRITING PROMPTS:

Writing for Purpose

Sometimes purpose in life is elusive. Without purpose, life just happens to us, and we have less control over the events that shape and direct the course our lives take. The following exercises are designed to help you self-examine your life as it is right now and take the control you need to direct it. They ask direct, sometimes confrontational questions of you, and you can expect to be challenged in answering them.

WEEK 45: EXISTENTIALISM

Existentialists believe that there is no inherent meaning or purpose to life. Without a set purpose, we create meaning and purpose for ourselves and often use that purpose as a guiding principle for how to go about our lives. In this exercise you'll be asked to examine your core beliefs and see what meaning you can create for your life. To start, jot down a list of your core beliefs. Write quickly without any sort of self-examination. Then look over the list. Does one of your core beliefs seem to pull you more strongly than the others? Spend a few minutes imagining how leading a life informed by and dedicated to your beliefs would look. Then write down how each of the beliefs you hold could impact your day-to-day life.

WEEK 46: SELF-REFLECTIVE WRITING EXERCISES

This series of questions will get you thinking about your current life and the direction you are headed. Make sure to complete these questions when you have some time to ponder the answers. First, take out a blank sheet of paper and answer the following questions:

How would you rank your current life on a scale of 1–10, where 1 is completely unsatisfactory and 10 is perfect? If you aren't close to a 10, what is preventing you from ranking it higher? What do you need to do to get to a 10?

According to James Pennebaker, the things that keep you lying awake at night are some of the most fruitful places to start writing. What keeps you tossing and turning at night?

Examining the things you want to avoid can bring you closer to understanding what steps you need to take to get to where you want to be. Ask yourself, what do I not want to discuss with anyone? What is it that I can't admit to myself? Why not?

Naikan is a Japanese method of self-examination. To practice Naikan, ask yourself the following questions: What have I gotten from someone? What have I gifted someone? What difficulties and tribulations have I caused this person?

Epictetus, a Greek Stoic philosopher, wrote that rather than wishing events would conform to our desires, we should make our desires conform to what is happening. What unwanted people, things, or events in your life can you try to "desire" or treat with more sympathy?

True freedom is the absence of fear. What are you most afraid of? Why? How would your life be different if you were free of fear?

Clarify Your Values

Imagine for a moment that you had unlimited confidence. Nothing could set you back on your path because your confidence level was at its peak. Answer the following statements:

- If I had unlimited confidence this is how I would treat people differently.
- This is how I would act differently.
- This is how I would treat myself differently.
- These are the personal character traits I would develop.
- Here is how I would treat family and close friends differently.
- Here is how I would treat coworkers and business associates differently.
- These are the important things I would stand for.
- I would start doing these activities.
- These are the goals I would try to meet.
- Here is how I would improve my life overall.

Next, take a sheet of paper and divide it into four parts. One for Health, one for Love, one for Play, and one for Work. Under each area of your life, write your core values down and set short-term, medium-term, and long-term goals for each area. Make sure you set a timeframe to achieve these goals.

WRITING PROMPTS:

Powerful

In these exercises, you'll free associate different purposes for your life. Make sure you have enough quiet time set aside to complete the activities. The first one, for instance, will take about forty-five minutes.

WEEK 47: WRITE IT OUT!

Take a blank piece of paper and write "What is my purpose in life?" at the top of it. Next, write whatever comes to mind—"I want to be a bricklayer," or whatever it is. Keep writing and writing, jotting down whatever comes to mind. After about twenty to thirty minutes, you may hit a slump and start thinking "This is stupid, why am I doing this?" Write that down as well, but circle any thoughts that seem to be powerful. After about thirty to forty minutes, you find yourself circling back to a theme that seems to fit your purpose in life. You may even get a clear mission statement. Spend some time thinking about how you can integrate the clear directives into your life.

Nietzsche wrote about the idea of eternal recurrence. That given the chance to relive our lives over and over again for eternity, we might make different choices about how we go about our days. We'd choose to avoid the painful occurrences and reap the benefits of the better parts of our days. How would you relive your life, given the chance? Take out a blank sheet of paper and think of a particular day where things did or did not go your way. Maybe it was a mixed bag kind of a day where some parts went smoothly and other parts were more difficult. What decisions would you make differently? Write it down. Thinking in this way can help you in your daily life by showing you that you have a list of choices to make each day that directly affect the outcome of your life.

Your Best Life

Imagining your best life can open pathways in your mind that will lead you to attaining it. It may not be *perfect*, but your imagination can bring you closer to achieving more of what you're looking for out of life. Imagine aspects of your life as if they were perfect, magical, and carefree.

Think about:

- **A Perfect Day:** Hopefully, you've experienced a perfect day in your lifetime. One of those days when everything just seems to go the right way with very little effort on your part, when you are happy and easy-going and there is no limit to how much you can accomplish. Imagine the perfect day for yourself.
- **Unconditional Love:** Unconditional love is something many people talk about, but it's rare to find it in the world today. It's a love without bounds or expectations that makes you feel stronger and more secure. What does unconditional love mean to you? How would it make you feel to be loved unconditionally? Describe this kind of love in your journal and write about how it feels to be loved unconditionally. Who in your life loves you unconditionally? Who do you love in this way?
- **A Perfect House:** If you could live anywhere, where would you live? What is in the yard? What amenities would make you happiest? Maybe it's a gas range, or a reading nook, set aside just for you. What kind of neighbors (if any) would live next door? What is your favorite room in the house? What would you do there?

Use Your Imagination

Dream big, because there is no limit to what you can envision. The bigger your dreams, the more likely you are to find a solid middle space somewhere between perfection and the life you are living right now.

WEEK 49: SELF-CARE VISION BOARD

You'll need a piece of poster board for this activity and anything you'd like to decorate your vision board with. In this exercise you'll start by brainstorming a list of self-care activities you can indulge in. Next, think of keywords or phrases that you can tie to each of these activities. Write them all down and then cut them out and post them to your poster board in a way that's pleasing to the eye. Hang your vision board in a place where you'll be reminded to take care of yourself.

WEEK 50: CREATIVE LICENSE

Sometimes, when you don't know the whole story behind an incident, it can trouble you with nagging thoughts and worries. In this exercise, you'll fill in the blanks to an incident you don't know the full story to, either because you weren't present, or because your memory of the event is poor. First, think of an incident that is hazy in your mind. Then think of all the things you've heard about what happened from different people. Then, write out the incident in full using the information you've been given to fill in the blanks. It's not really fiction if you are using other witness testimony to extrapolate what happened.

How to Encourage Confidence in Others

Systemic racism works, in part, because it undermines Black people's sense of self-worth and achievement. Fighting racism requires you to be vigilant on many fronts and encouraging others to feel strong is one of the many ways you can fight racism. Young Black girls especially need to be reminded to believe in themselves. Sometimes young girls can struggle with jealousy and bullying. It's better to be supportive of each other and give a hand up to those who have fallen on hard times. Encouraging confidence in your friends and those you encounter will do a great deal to boost your own self-esteem and self-confidence. You may find that encouraging confidence is a daily struggle for you, especially if your friends have been bullied or picked on. Keep trying to encourage their confidence anyway. Here are some tips for building self-confidence:

Make sure your friends know that your love is unconditional. Don't withhold love if they do something differently than you would like; let them know you'll love them no matter what. Make sure you fill them with the love the world around them won't always provide, do your best to let them know they are capable, loved, and, most importantly, free. Having the freedom to make their own choices doesn't mean that you will allow yourself to be mistreated, however. It just means that you respect your friends and won't hold their personal decisions against them.

Schedule time with them to do fun things that you both enjoy, and practice positive self-talk; this might seem a little awkward at first, but when you hear them say something like, "I'm so stupid," stop them and encourage them to talk positively to and about themselves.

Praise your friends the right way. Praise them in a way that acknowledges their choices and actions. Tell them, "I like the way you blocked that goal," not, "You are the best goalie who ever lived!" Let them overhear you saying positive things about them to other people; don't brag, but do mention notable achievements to other people within earshot.

Don't be intimidated by your friends' emotions. It is especially important for Black kids and young adults to know they're allowed to feel sad and cry, and they should be encouraged to open up about these feelings. There is a tendency in the Black community to "toughen up," because we know how cruel the world can be. We encourage people to eat their feelings a lot, but feelings get hurt—it's a part of life. When you allow your friends to express their negative emotions, you allow yourself to be a fully-feeling human as well. Encourage them to connect with their emotions and express their feelings by asking, "How does that make you feel?" This will help build an honest, open relationship between the two of you.

What do you do if your non-Black friends keep saying the wrong things about racism?

It can be difficult for non-Black people to talk about racism. The subject has been taboo for many of them for most of their lives, and they are just learning the vocabulary to clearly and openly speak up about racism. And we *want* non-Black people to speak out about racism. But what do you do if your friends just don't get it right? What if they insist that "all lives matter"?

Get better friends.

Ha! Just kidding. But remember, first, it's not your responsibility to educate non-Black people on racism. If non-Black people are sincere in wanting to find out more, they can do the research themselves, and constantly fielding questions or trying to raise awareness can wear you out and may have some psychological repercussions.

The best thing you can do is be honest about how racism impacts you and raise awareness of why what these friends are saying is hurtful. For example, "All lives matter." You can tell them that all lives *should* matter, but that Black people are killed in racist actions more often than any other race, and so until Black Lives Matter equally, "All lives matter" is not a true statement. You can tell them how it makes you feel when they continue to say, "All lives matter." But come at it from the standpoint of raising awareness, not educating them or telling them how to behave.

In this portion of his public post, Brian Crooks relates the frustration of living under systemic racism: "White people often say that we make everything about race. That's because, for us, damn near everything *is* about race. It's always been that way."

If you feel someone is really trying to learn, you may want to cut them some slack, but if they are hard-lined about the issue, it may be best to let them go, and focus your energy elsewhere.

Reframe Your Perspective

Before you even begin looking for ways to build your friends' self-esteem, consider how you feel about yourself. How healthy is your self-esteem? If your self-esteem is low, ask yourself why, and start to strategize ways you can boost it. No one is perfect. We all have flaws, but understanding that if you are weak in some areas, you probably possess strengths in others will help bring some balance into your sense of self. It is important that you watch yourself when talking to others. If you say things like, "I'm so stupid," you are sending a message that it's okay to talk down about yourself, and it isn't.

Your internal dialogue is a big part of what makes up your sense of self. Start looking for solutions instead of obsessing about mistakes. Say you repeatedly get a parking ticket at a place you visit regularly. Rather than telling yourself that you're a failure, start putting a roll of quarters in the car so you can pay the parking meter, and praise yourself when you remember to pay the meter. Simple steps like that will help you build self-esteem a little at a time.

When you have a negative mindset, it's hard to believe in yourself and that good things can and will happen to you. If you are stuck in the thought pattern that you don't deserve good things, or that you just can't, you are inviting negativity into your life. One way to deal with a negative mindset is to reframe your perspective. Words are magical in the sense that they can shape our reality, and how you speak to yourself matters, so you want to choose your words wisely. The journaling prompts for this week will help you reframe your thinking pattern and invite prosperity and joy into your life.

WEEK 51: RE-AUTHORING

In this exercise you'll look at a problem closely and try to find positives in it or reframe the narrative you're using to describe the problem into one that is more positive and fits with your essential values. Start by describing the problem in detail. Then ask yourself the following questions and write out your responses:

- How did you intend the situation to unfold? What was the purpose of your actions?
- What values or beliefs do these actions support?
- What hopes and dreams are associated with these values?
- What principles of living are supported by these hopes and dreams?
- What commitment have you made to stand behind these principles of living as demonstrated by your actions?

Next, rewrite the problem as a statement of your commitment to principles of living. How can you resolve the problem without sacrificing these principals?

WEEK 52: REFRAMING IRRATIONAL THOUGHTS

Irrational thoughts and mind traps can take many forms. "I must be perfect, or no one will like me." "Other people must be perfect, or they are no good." They can take many different forms, such as:

- Magnifying: Making a problem much bigger than it is in reality.
- Minimizing: Underestimating the importance of something.
- Filtering: Focusing only on the negative aspects of a situation.
- Jumping to conclusions: Interpreting an event or situation without examining the facts of the situation.
- Personalization: Making a situation or incident all about you and ignoring other people's needs and responsibility to the situation.
- All or Nothing Thinking: Seeing a situation as black-and-white without understanding the nuances.
- Overgeneralization: Seeing a brief incident as a never-ending source of failure or a complete defeat.
- Emotional Reasoning: Using your emotions to gauge the truth of a situation.

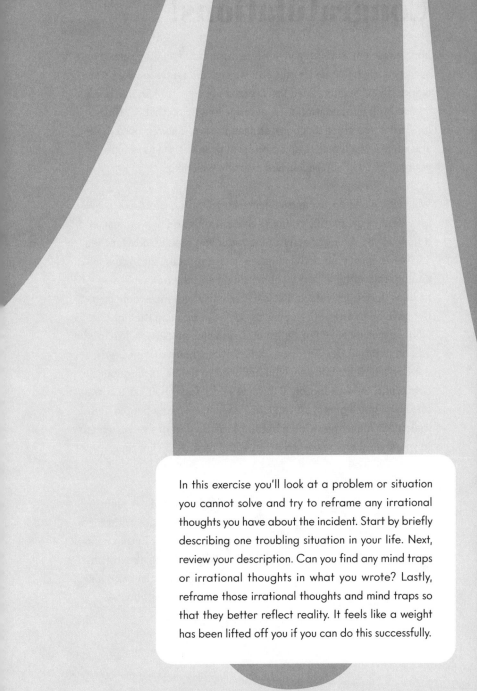

In this exercise you'll look at a problem or situation you cannot solve and try to reframe any irrational thoughts you have about the incident. Start by briefly describing one troubling situation in your life. Next, review your description. Can you find any mind traps or irrational thoughts in what you wrote? Lastly, reframe those irrational thoughts and mind traps so that they better reflect reality. It feels like a weight has been lifted off you if you can do this successfully.

Congratulations!

You've made it through a year of learning more about yourself and society. I hope you feel confident, strong, and ready to take on the world. If you've completed the exercises and lessons in this book, you've built a foundation for a practice in writing that continues long after you close this book and set it down on your bookshelf—and I hope you'll pick it up again from time to time to remind yourself of what you've learned over the past year.

With images of unrest and violence surrounding protests prevalent in the media, you may be hesitant to go to a protest, and it may not be the right activity for you if you aren't ready for that. Whatever form your activism takes, it is important that you have an understanding of why people protest and the impact it can have. Without protests and acts of civil disobedience, there might not have been any of the advances we have made in the fight against racism: No Civil Rights Act, no voter protection. We might still be living under Jim Crow laws. Representative John Lewis, the Civil Rights champion who marched in Selma, throughout the South, and in Washington, DC, once said, "You only pass this way once, you gotta give it all you can." It will take many people giving their all to make the world a better place. Be part of the movement in whatever way you can contribute and recognize that there's a lot you *can* do.

Activism isn't limited to protests about racism; there are plenty of causes worth fighting for, some of which intersect with anti-racist protests. There are many activities you can take part in that make a difference. There are also plenty of young activists, like the ones mentioned in this chapter, who find ways to fight racism and for other causes on their own terms, using their own methods.

You could:

- Educate and read
- Attend a town hall
- Advocate for Legislation/Engage civically
- Run for office
- Protest
- Create a public awareness campaign that includes social media / Pick up the digital pen
- Support those on the ground
- Do a survey about the issue and share the results
- Raise/Donate money
- Write a letter to a company
- Call out the behavior of racists
- Engage in community service
- Get the press involved
- Practice self-care
- Be joyful and hopeful
- Support marginalized-owned businesses
- Create
- Find what works for you

Whether you choose to start your own initiative or help out one that's already in place, you have a lot of choices to select from. The world needs as much help as it can get, so do your part to make it a better place.

Hopefully by now, you've become comfortable with freewriting and will turn to your journal to help you figure out the world around, which is an often-confusing overwhelming place, especially for Black girls and young women.

It is my hope that you will become part of a growing movement of brilliant leaders who believe in the possibility of a better, more prosperous future for Black girls. It is important for you to connect with a community of like-minded thinkers, who will keep you motivated and empowered to make change in your own life and in your community. The Badass Black Girl website (badassblackgirl. com) is a great resource for interviews and blog articles designed to help keep you informed, up to date, and inspired. I hope you'll follow the blog and continue fighting for justice and equality.

—M.J.

About the Author

Born in Port-au-Prince, Haiti, **M.J. Fievre** moved to the United States in 2002. She currently writes from Miami.

M.J.'s publishing career began as a teenager in Haiti. At nineteen years old, she signed her first book contract with Hachette-Deschamps in Haiti for the publication of a young adult book titled *La Statuette Maléfique*. Since then, M.J. has authored nine books in French that are widely read in Europe and the French Antilles. In 2013, One Moore Book released M.J.'s first children's book, *I Am Riding*, written in three languages: English, French, and Haitian Creole. In 2015, Beating Windward Press published M.J.'s memoir, *A Sky the Color of Chaos*, about her childhood in Haiti during the brutal regime of Jean-Bertrand Aristide.

M.J. Fievre is the author of *Happy, Okay? Poems about Anxiety, Depression, Hope, and Survival* (Books & Books Press, 2019) and *Badass Black Girl: Questions, Quotes, and Affirmations for Teens* (Mango Publishing, 2020). She helps others write their way through trauma, build community, and create social change. She works with veterans, disenfranchised youth, cancer patients and survivors, victims of domestic and sexual violence, minorities, the elderly, those with chronic illness or going through transitions, and any underserved population in need of writing as a form of therapy— even if they don't realize that they need writing or therapy.

A long-time educator and frequent keynote speaker (Tufts University, Massachusetts; Howard University, Washington, DC; the University of Miami, Florida; and Michael College, Vermont; and a panelist at the Association of Writers & Writing Programs Conference, AWP), M.J. is available for book club meetings, podcast presentations, interviews, and other author events.

Contact M.J. at 954-391-3398 or email happyokay@gmail.com.

Mango Publishing, established in 2014, publishes an eclectic list of books by diverse authors—both new and established voices—on topics ranging from business, personal growth, women's empowerment, LGBTQ studies, health, and spirituality to history, popular culture, time management, decluttering, lifestyle, mental wellness, aging, and sustainable living. We were recently named 2019 *and* 2020's #1 fastest-growing independent publisher by *Publishers Weekly*. Our success is driven by our main goal, which is to publish high quality books that will entertain readers as well as make a positive difference in their lives.

Our readers are our most important resource; we value your input, suggestions, and ideas. We'd love to hear from you—after all, we are publishing books for you!

Please stay in touch with us and follow us at:

Facebook: Mango Publishing
Twitter: @MangoPublishing
Instagram: @MangoPublishing
LinkedIn: Mango Publishing
Pinterest: Mango Publishing
Newsletter: mangopublishinggroup.com/newsletter

Join us on Mango's journey to reinvent publishing, one book at a time.